DEATH, POLITICS, AND THE HUBRIS OF CONSCIOUSNESS

Politics and Psychoanalysis

Bruce F. Grube

UNIVERSITY
PRESS OF
AMERICA

Library of Congress Catalog Card Number: **81-40600**

To Kathryn

ACKNOWLEGMENTS

While I, of course, assume responsibility for this book, particularly its errors, it is not, in the strictest sense, my work, but belongs also to those who have influenced me and to who I am indebted for their ideas and support. First of all, I thank my parents, Katharine Gannon and Bruce W. Grube for nurturing me and seeing to my education, and especially for keeping television away from our home until I had developed a love for reading and reflection. Neither one, I suspect, ever thought their son would write a book of so little interest to so many. I thank Sri Krishna Menon for general understanding reflected throughout, and particularly in the chapter concerning causality. Several academic colleagues have figured in my ideas as well: Prof. Harry Hall interested me in political sociology; Prof. Herbert Hirsch provided invaluable comments upon my work, friendship, and cold beer now and again; Prof. Richard Kraemer, is friend and contributor in general; Prof. Louis Zurcher stimulated my interest in social psychology; Prof. Roderick Bell interested me in C. G. Jung and the politics of knowledge; Prof. Raja Rao added significantly to my philosophical education; Prof. Jose Vadi discussed many of the ideas contained in this work with me and is a good friend; Prof. Stanley Rothman retained his sense of humor while allowing me to debate the relative merits of Freud and Jung with him and also commented extensively upon this manuscript which was of great assistance to me; Alex Hill, M.D., Jungian analyst and teacher; and, Jon Hart Olson engaged me in many influential conversations, although I have not yet forgiven him for not following through on a planned European trip (there is no truth to the rumor that he is Anthony Burgess' model for Carlo Campanati). Late-hour philosophical conversations and motorcycle rides with my friend Billy Bob Willms provided not only pleasure, but many ideas. Marc Adin, Kathy Adin, Kathy Marcus, John Kunz, Kenneth and Virginia Moore, Gloria Moore Abbott, Artie Meyer, Hope Sanford, Kathryn Starnes, Delfy Vadi, Brian Worley, and many others gave me discussion, friendship, humor and care, often contributing unknowingly, but most generously to my work. With these people I have shared laughter and tears. Mert Starnes graciously let me use the study of his home in Austin for the final preparation of this manuscript. I thank Frances Woods for typing and editing the form of the manuscript. Her assistance was excellent, although she still feels my paragraphs are too long. My tendency, I maintain, toward lengthy paragraphs is genetic in nature. Finally, I thank the National Endowment for the Humanities which provided funds that allowed me to work in part on this book in the summer of 1979 at Smith College, Northampton.

B.F.G.

Palmer Canyon
Claremont, California
1981

TABLE OF CONTENTS

PREFACE

We have lingered in the chambers of the sea
By sea-girls wreathed with seaweed red and brown
Till human voices wake us, and we drown.
—T. S. Eliot

Politics in our time is a politics of fear. Any cursory exploration of current domestic or international politics with its potential for destruction and domination would reveal this character. Psychologically, it is a politics which has arisen due to the splitting off of the unconscious from the conscious mind; from the exclusion of the nonrational from our analyses of human nature. To examine this problem and its consequences, I have mainly used the perspective of Jungian psychology, a not oft-used or understood view in the academic social sciences, because it offers the possibility of going to the essence, to the core of the question. Several related themes are raised throughout the discussion in the following essay which are elements of the general question and which I will enumerate briefly. Notwithstanding, I wish to point out that the nature of the question I have chosen to probe is not readily susceptible to enumeration and I have, therefore, intentionally fallen upon what may appear at first glance to be a discursive style of writing. For those readers who think I am circuitous, dialectical, or even didactic, I thank you for your observations and readily admit my guilt, for I know human nature is best and most accurately described in paradoxical, and sometimes dramatic, fashion.

Chapter one argues that the social sciences have lost the perspective necessary for understanding because they have lost touch with what it means to be human largely due to an uncritical imitating of the methodologies of the natural sciences and the positing of rational theories which have but little connection to the way life is actually lived. This chapter also contains an analysis of the application of socialization theory to human behavior in the social sciences and shows that it rests upon an irrational base. There exists a "politics of knowledge" which should be more thoroughly studied and brought into relation with prevalent theory.

Chapter two is a depth analysis of causality and probability. Again, this is an effort to demonstrate that the very essence of the foundation upon which positivist theory is built is itself illusory. In chapter three, I have briefly outlined the essentials of Jungian psychology in order to tie together the elements presented in chapters one and two, and to provide a framework for expanding upon the relationship between the fear of death, Phobos, and immortalizing activity, including the politics of knowledge, which is manifest in the production of intellectual theories and the emergence of mass man. Fear of death underlies the sublimation and diffusion of politics which is to be found in academic theory as well as in mass society.

ix

Chapters four and five are descriptions of the connection between Phobos and politics, and focus upon authoritarianism, dogmatism, alienation, individualism, mass society, and nonparticipation. The final chapter is a summation and somewhat self-conscious urging toward a reconceptualization of human nature in the social sciences which should proceed inseparably with self-examination if we are to realize integration in our theories or ourselves, and community in our political life.

CHAPTER I

HUMAN NATURE AND CONTEMPORARY SOCIAL SCIENCE:
The Loss of Perspective

> . . . we can no longer appeal to the narrowly
> intellectual, scientific standpoint . . .
>
> - C. G. Jung[1]

Perhaps all human beings require illusions of some sort to seemingly soften their lives. It is certainly well known that the human ego is fragile and is often well bulwarked. Social scientists are no exception to this observation and may, in actuality, be even more susceptible to the temptation of masking reality with rationalities which have only the barest connection to their own existences than those people who do not spend so much of their time explicitly wrapped about by intricate abstractions. Yet, it is also the case that all humans imprison themselves in their illusions and so it is more accurate to say that the social scientist is only a special case of that which is actually a life problem. A depth exploration would reveal the substance of this problem. For example, the human nature of the social scientist, in reality, underlies the social scientist's exploration of the human nature of others. This is a paradox of the highest magnitude, but it is also one of the least explored in the contemporary literature. This is understandable in a sense for any penetrating examination of the paradox would involve one also in a profound examination of oneself. It may very well be that it feels safer, in the short run at least, to stand behind the scarecrows sheltering oneself from this examination.

The most significant illusions involve the nature of human nature because they ultimately involve each individual. The social scientist cannot avoid this. It is not possible to study human beings in association or singly without intellectually constructing assumptions or formulating conceptions about the "nature" of human nature. Yet, the totality of human nature cannot be understood merely by intellect. For those who study human beings, there will always remain an intellectual assumption of course, however remote and implicit, concerning human nature which will serve as the foundation for their theories and ideas. No particular theory, frame of reference, or methodology escapes this fact. It is also the case, examining the dominant literature within the social sciences, that the concept of human nature, rather than being full and rich, is a narrow one which has been stripped of its subjective and non-rational character. It is my contention that this narrow notion of human nature has become a scarecrow designed to frighten away ideas which would suggest that human nature cannot actually be reduced to rational concepts, theories, or operational definitions.

1

It is not, I would like to stress, my point here to claim that rationality should be abandoned or that an anti-intellectual stance should be adopted, but rather that the rational view must be balanced by the complement of non-rationality. If one fails to see both poles at once, then the conscious-rational idea becomes inflated, thinking that the actual nature of human beings has been, or will be, grasped and known. It is then that human nature as articulated by the social scientific literature in general resembles little that is fully human. Human nature, instead, becomes shrunken to a mere expression of the intellectual function which is a partial of human nature. All of us, in a strict sense, are worse and better people than such emaciated theories would have us believe.

The inflation of the rational view has resulted in a reification accompanied by a loss of perspective in the social sciences which can be restored, not through an abandonment of rational or intellectual effort, but through a respect for that which is non-rational, non-measureable, and non-predictable. In this manner "humaness" can consciously emerge in our studies and perspective could be gained. This process would involve a critical examination of social scientific assumptions. This task could hardly be a negative endeavor, since an unexamined social science seems hardly worth pursuing in the first place. Obscuring the paradoxical and unconscious aspects of human nature, as is the wont of contemporary social science, does not bring the understandings which would illumine human nature, but engages us in an uncritical and abstract world with its own dangers. The failure to see the paradox will undoubtedly result eventually in cultural anti-intellectualism as the rationality of the social sciences is taken to an extreme. In this sense, the social sciences are largely self-destructive and blind to the unconscious problem they have created for themselves. We may be assured that anti-intellectualism will not be seen by social scientists as having any origin in themselves, but rather as residing solely in the uneducated mass.

The foundation of this world of abstraction remains the rational conceptualization of the human self. The social scientific conceptualization of human nature is simply insufficient. All behaviorally oriented literature—and one might add, any analysis purporting to explicate human beings, their environment, or the processes of interaction between a human being and the environment—explicitly or implicitly, involves a conceptualization, a thought, about the human self, about human nature. Thus, it becomes necessary to understand the implications of the conceptualizing faculty of the human mind so as to be able to portray as faithful a picture of the reality and life of human nature as is possible, given what is obviously a paradoxical situation. How is experience represented?

The concept, "the self" or "personality," is, illustratively, a rational abstraction used to denote what is, in actuality, immediate and non-abstract. Examined closely, any concept of human nature ultimately dissolves into reality. When political scientists refer to the self, even in an abstract way, they are, in a particular sense, unwittingly referring to themselves for they are human beings. The concept of the self has

2

reference to the networks by which an individual as social scientist will filter or form reality into abstraction. These networks are both psychological and physical, they can be of the intellectual and sensual functions of the psyche as they are manifested in thought and feeling, of a learned symbolic nature, or they may relate to what we know as seemingly more concrete physical or biological grids. They more often than not remain unconscious, for the reflection necessary to come to terms with the unconscious may prove arduous and seemingly without immediate practical benefit.

One might suggest that the personal pronoun "I" could be substituted for "the self" when that concept is used by a social scientist interested in human political behavior. This throws the problem back to the social scientist where it properly belongs. After all, if one cannot understand one's own nature, then how is it possible to understand the nature of others? One cannot give enlightenment which one does not really have. The paradox of the human self examining the human self would, in this case, have been made conscious and explicit, rather than buried in the objectified theoretics of the abstract "self" which render the vital aspects of human nature unconscious. Now the question simply becomes: To whom does the personal pronoun "I" refer? Do social scientists understand what "I" represents or means? Can one know what "I" represents or means? Since subject and object are complements, can one, therefore, know what "it" means? Do we ultimately know or understand human nature?

Here it will be argued that one cannot ultimately "know" either the origins or the terminations of human nature. And this fact must be taken into account in order to faithfully portray human activity. That is, scientific rationality simply cannot be applied to large areas of human experience—particularly those areas which are not susceptible to rational explanation or measurement. This essay is concerned with the hubris of consciousness and addresses that problem by examining the nature of knowledge concerning human nature, its relationship to the search for personal and collective immortality and the fear of death underlying that search. In brief, the arrogance of an unbridled and unwise rationality is an element in the complex originating in Phobos, the fear of death—the fear that there is nothing if rationality as the vision of reality is sacrificed. Yet, it is precisely this sacrifice which must be offered in order to not only know, but also to understand human existence. The alternative is to live in dread of the unconscious as it seeps into and sometimes floods our most careful rational conscious constructions, dealing death to a world we conceived. The fear of death is the symbol of the consequence of assimilating the unconscious to ego consciousness. Phobos, in the guise of rationalization, authoritarianism, alienation, dogmatism, and rigidity arises as neurotic unconscious elements engaged in immortalizing activity. In this light one should ask, how is authentic study possible at all? How can science proceed? How can intellectual work be done?

3

Science, first of all, is knowing. It is one's experimentation in the world. Ignorance or curiosity may be the motivation of such experimentation, however, the rigid adoption of a particular methodology or view, such as science as empiricism, merely represents the doctrinaire choice of a frame of reference within an infinite range of frames of reference by which one might know something, it is the adoption of an account. The intentional use of "psyche" within this essay is a means of breaking away from an account, the polarized reference of the social scientific "self." Psyche refers at once to both consciousness and unconsciousness; the rational and non-rational. It is an attempt to refer to the totality of human nature rather than to an account. C. G. Jung, in speaking to the concept of the ego, describes the problem which actually faces social scientists who accept the conventional reference of the empirical ego.

> As a conscious fact the ego could, theoretically at least, be described completely. But this would never amount to more than a picture of the conscious personality; all those features which are unknown or unconscious to the subject would be missing. A total description of the personality is, even in theory, absolutely impossible, because the unconscious portion of it cannot be grasped cognitively.[2]

This problem of adequately representing the human self will be explored psychoanalytically and philosophically because this perspective is an expression which embraces the total nature. Attentiveness will be given to the paradoxical character, not only of consciousness in political activity, but also to the unconscious sources of political activity, to the random, the unknown, the non-rational, the uncertain--the ephemerae of the human psyche which will always belong to the realm of the essentially mysterious. The unsolved, irresolvable, transformational view will complement and bring a more accurate picture of the human being than the representations of an unbalanced rational theory. More wisdom is contained in the paradox, or complementarity, than in the meaningless precision of linear, mathematical, or numerical studies, for it acknowledges the limits of cognitive activity and rescues us from the arrogance of pride which would doom us in our search for truth.

The use of science in the social sciences has come to be a narrow-minded enterprise in need of a wider vision. The products of the scientific method are currently valued more highly than understanding the origins of science and its relationship to human spontaneity and creativity. Philosophy, literature, poetry and art find little place in modern social science departments. The products of the scientific method are valued over such "subjective" understandings of human nature because they seem to confer control and power over the environment--in fact, over the "world," and therefore, one might say, control over Phobos itself. While these contentions will be elaborately discussed throughout the chapters of this essay, it will no doubt prove helpful to briefly state the problems: first, the concern with the products of rational science has led to a view which construes science as a means. Science is a "thing" from which control and power may be gotten; second, this perspective of science has meant that metaphysical questions concerning the sources of science, of hypotheses, and so forth, have been cut off; third, concern with understanding human beings has been diminished by the elimination of the subjective and metaphysical questions concerning sources and meaning, while knowledge about human behavior has been abundantly increased. Metaphysical questions, we must keep in mind, are always psychologically grounded, thus ignoring or diminishing the philosophical, as an arena of the unsolvable, in turn diminishes human psychology to the level of an interesting game at best and a tedious dogma shedding scant light on the human condition at worst.[3] The quest for rational theory, method and technique is an ironic one. Inasmuch as exclusively rational theory, method and technique are regarded as science, those who possess such a view are actually involved in the destruction of science--they are engaged in scientism which excludes the genius emerging from an unhabitual manner of seeing the world and oneself.

Since scientism, as employed within the social and behavioral sciences, seeks to eradicate mystery, to obscure the level of complementarity, to describe human nature, and eliminate uncertainty, it must, as an intellectual strategy, or methodology, retain a deficient status with regard to understanding human phenomena. Human nature is paradoxical as we shall see. Behavioral explanations, on the other hand, which view human beings as bounded by their skins and defined by "behaviors," and striving for consistency, are only very narrowly correct. For example, while humans express consistency in their natures, they, at the same time, also express the non-consistent and are attracted by the novel, even though that which is novel may have been repressed. The study of human nature has, in the behavioral view, largely taken a vision in which ego-consciousness, as it were, has been reified in the study of human phenomena as if it were the totality. The exploration of human nature is, in this sense, founded upon a mistake with considerable consequences for the social sciences. As social scientists it may be difficult, but perhaps to ourselves, we can at least approach the problem in our most private moments when persona is useless and admit that we really do not know what the "I" is, and therefore, do not ultimately know why or who we are or what the "it" is. And perhaps the danger in that is that we remain unamused by this seemingly chaotic and uncertain prospect and long to be where everything is clear in order to avoid the seeming nothingness which must underlie all rationalisms. It is in this sense that the study of politics is the study of rational ego-consciousness and the study of national politics is the study of collective ego-consciousness, thus we often do not see our own shadow even though it falls upon the objects of our studies.

In formulating a depth analysis, the view taken by C. G. Jung of the human psyche has been largely adopted in the present study as an open mood from which to consider human nature. This is an approach which is both rational and non-rational at once. Jung is, without doubt, a seminal figure in Twentieth Century theory and yet his work has been

5

introverted, and then the chief value lies with the subject and his relation to the idea. In the former case, culture takes on a collective character, in the latter an individual one.[5]

American culture is of the collective character at the substantive level while appearing to stress the individual, particularly through the ideology of individualism, at the "symbolic" level. This tends to render the subjective complement unconscious. To the social scientist, of course, the subject, the self, seemingly is addressed. But the address is rational and the focus as a consequence is "self as object." Additionally, our time can be described as bureaucratized (including the production of knowledge), rational, and technological. In general, therefore, our researches tend to typify our condition rather than explain it. One area of behavioral study, socialization, pays a great deal of attention to human nature and creates the impression that it can offer explanations as to human activity. This is an example of such typification. An examination of socialization theory will demonstrate the reification problems which have been discussed to this point.

Socialization—"Humans as a Product of Environment"

Socialization studies have attempted to understand political and social phenomena from a rational perspective, neglecting the unconscious in formulating models of human nature. Underlying the concern with socialization, and the socialized individual, is a set of implicit questions which reflect conscious concern with rationality and avoidance of non-rationality and uncertainty. These questions occur in various forms, but notably in the study of politics, for example, they have to do with the nature of political order, authority, and cohesion. What are the sources of political order? How is political order and society possible? How does a human being become managed in terms of systemic social and political rules? Then, assuming that men are capable of "accepting" the rules of the game, the additional question arises as to how highly differentiated social and political systems deter and organize destructive antagonisms between groups.

The answers to the question of how political order is possible among human beings, in terms of socialization, have been framed, in their fundamental forms, in two general ways: first, internal formulations based upon the notion of the internalization of norms; and second, external emphases based in the notion that people are motivated by the desire to win favor with others, by gaining acceptance, status, and prestige. It should be clearly noted that both of these models, however, are based on "external" observation of "behaviors" and are rationalistic and extroverted in character. Sociologist Dennis Wrong notes that the first conceptualization assumes that society controls the individual from the outside by imposing sanctions upon the person and thus constraining one, while the second view assumes that social rules are not only external in nature, but become internal, psychological, and thus, self-imposed.[6]

This assumption about the behavior of people creates a perspective which is misleading, for it argues that human social behavior is totally shaped by cultural norms or patterns which have been institutionalized. Illustratively, Clyde Kluckhohn stated that

> a definition of socialization in any culture is the predictability of an individual's daily behavior in various defined situations. When a person behaves most of the time as others do in following cultural routines, he is then socialized.[7]

or, F. Elkin,

> the process by which someone learns the ways of a given society or social group well enough so that he can function with it.[8]

or, D. F. Aberle,

> Socialization consists of those patterns of action or aspects of action which inculcate in individuals the skills (including knowledge), motives and attitudes necessary for the performance of present or anticipated roles.[9]

It seems obvious that socialization and predictability (social control) are of the same mold. Simply put, these scholars maintain that behaviors which conform to norms are rewarded, and those which violate norms are punished. There is, of course, despite the literature, no absolute distinction in reality between these two fundamental tendencies conceptualizing human nature in the socialization scholarship. But, implicit in this first tendency is the problem of how, given this framework, can one account for violence, revolution, conflict or one's personal notion of social and political systemic coercion. These questions could not exist if the human psyche, in actuality, was shaped completely by norms and institutionalized designs—if "human nature" were not more mysterious and uncertain than socialization theorists are willing to admit. Perhaps an element of human nature may be addressed in a qualified way by socialization theory, but not human nature itself.

Taking the theoretical pattern found in socialization literature concerning internalization, one finds that internalization has come to be identified with learning. That is to say, when a social rule is "internalized" by a person, he or she conforms to it in terms of observable behaviors—he or she has "learned" it. "Behavior," of course, can be observed, so it would seem, and such observation serves to "validate" the inference of internalization which is itself unobservable. Concern with political and social order underlies much of the political socialization literature, a view with which most socialization scholars would be in agreement. An example of the concern with order is evident when David Easton and Jack Dennis speak of the "socialization of support" which "contributes to the capacity of a political system to persist."[10] Setting aside for the moment the question of whether the fact of society actually needs "support," in terms of political socialization and learning theory in the first place, the relationship between conformity and internalization is assumed. By way of illustration, one can find the following passage in a well-known textbook on social psychology:

> In any event the content of culture is internalized through identification with parents and set up within the child's personality as a socializing and moral agency.[11]

Thus, a person, having "internalized" the rules, finds a need to conform to avoid the pain of a guilty conscience. It may very well be, however, that the double-bind involved in conforming may produce more anxiety for the conformer than for the individual who breaks the rules. Freud, from the perspective of psychoanalysis, remarked quite appropriately that,

> The more righteous a man is, the stricter and more suspicious will his conscience be, so that ultimately it is precisely those people who have carried holiness farthest who reproach themselves with the deepest sinfulness.[12]

So, one might postulate that anxiety may develop less severely in a person who seeks transcendence of social and political norms than the person who never breaks the moral or rational configuration and represses inner life. The psychoanalytic view in general, and Jung's view specifically, of human nature as more than behaviors leaves room for nondeterministic understandings. Jung's vision is not one which can be completely measured and predicted, although he certainly acknowledges the role of socialization as partial explanation. In the depth view, the experiencing of imagination, dreams, wishes, fantasies, myths, rituals, and emotions are all significant. Yet, to epitomize the position taken by many social science scholars, Lewis Froman dismisses the depth, "psychoanalytic" view by stating, rather arbitrarily, that,

(1) it draws attention away from possible agents of learning other than parents, such as peer groups, mass media, and school sources . . .

(2) it has not been adequately tested.

(3) more importantly, it tends to blend together the component parts of what have been referred to as "images" at the cost of theorizing about the learning process.[13]

This kind of criticism can be approached in several manners. To begin, Froman does not specify what he means by "psychoanalytic hypothesis," although one can imagine that he really means Sigmund Freud, who, despite the contemporary preponderance of "Freudians," does not represent all psychoanalytic thought; and, furthermore, one finds that in any case "neo-Freudians" have departed, in some cases substantially, from Freud's psychoanalytic theory, as in the cases of Erich Fromm, Karen Horney, Herbert Marcuse, and many others. In addition, psychoanalytic theory recognizes the influence of environmental encounters upon the manifest form of more basic patterns and conflicts which are contents of the psyche. To continue, what, then, does Froman mean by "adequately tested?" What would be the test? What would be adequate?--the application of the empirical method? The problem here would be how to test a theory which subsumes the theory which maintains the validity of the test itself. This problem cannot be ignored if one is truly being scientific. And, finally, one must recognize that "images," Froman's third point, are the basis for Froman's own work. His own model or image of human nature is necessary to his researches in political socialization. Images, in this sense, are part of objective experience--nations could not, for example, fight wars without an image of the "enemy" and "national security," and political scientists would not have students without images of "the government," "democracy," "pluralism," and so forth.

Images cannot be dismissed simply because they do not meet the exigencies of a particular methodology. And this, of course, is precisely the rub. Jung addresses this directly by observing that:

> The psyche consists essentially of images. It is a series of images in the truest sense, not an accidental juxtaposition or sequence, but a structure that is throughout full of meaning and purpose; it is a "picturing" of vital activities. And just as the material of the body that is ready for life has need of the psyche in order to be capable of life, so the psyche presupposes the living body in order that its images may live.[14]

It is also clearly the case that "theorizing" often has much to do with the knowledge of a person, but little to do with the understanding of a human nature. Additionally, "theorizing," as it is generally applied within the behavioral scholarship in the social sciences, means the utilization of the scientific methodology and philosophy which sustained Newtonian mechanics, but not contemporary science. The problem is complicated by the fact that those who ask metaphysical and non-rational questions are accused of being too theoretical, philosophical, and not objective, as though those who choose a particular approach currently in vogue are objective. However, when one cuts off metaphysical questions thereby sundering relationship to the unconscious, to the unknown and uncertain, one is merely engaging in a methodological ideology, a politics of knowledge, which is so far removed from life that it is only intellectual, abstract and hypothetical. The rejection of the depth view of human nature on this basis by Froman is, at best, "poor science." It is possibly, at worst, dogmatism; a system of belief about human nature so as to reduce its mystery to a known so that relief may be found from uncertainty. It is rational hubris and its unconscious complement needs to be brought into the light. People also learn from what their environment is not.

The second assumption found in the socialization literature by Wrong, although not always explicitly, is that people are motivated by the desire to win the favor of others. This, too, deserves additional analysis. Since the concepts which seek to represent the human psyche are not altogether susceptible to rational inquiry, political scientists interested in behavior have placed emphasis on the notion that the behavior of individuals is motivated by the expectations of others. This emphasis has been both implicit and, often, explicit:

> People are so profoundly sensitive to the expectations of others that all action is inevitably guided by those expectations.[15]

or,

> Groups can function smoothly only if the individuals who fill particular roles "learn their lines" and perform more or less as expected . . .[16]

or,

> The need for eliciting favorable responses from others is an almost constant component of (personality). Indeed, it is not too much to say that there is very little organized human behavior which is not directed toward its satisfaction in at least some degree.[17]

The concern with external factors in socialization allows for the inference of motives such as acceptance-seeking. Why would reinforcement by a parent modify behavior in a child? Such questions, from which acceptance-seeking can be inferred, have led to other concepts utilized by the socialization studies such as: peer groups; reference groups; significant others; and so forth. This is the sociological counterpart to the maximization of profit in capitalist economic theory.

The concepts of "rewards," "reinforcers," "pleasure," or "satisfiers," are linked to his notion of the acceptance-seeking person. At the aggregate level of conceptualization, of course, acceptance-seeking may become "value consensus." Basic tenets of learning theory,[18] the foundation for formulations of political socialization, are narcissistic in character, and view human behavior as a function of payoffs. Indeed, many of the rationalist investigations, especially those steeped in statistical methodology, which treat of voting behavior, violence, and so forth,[19] conceptualize behavior in terms of amount and kind of reward, payoff, and the potential punishment involved. These studies are founded on a lop-sided notion of human nature which a closer examination would

10

reveal. The questions of order, authority, cohesion, adaptation and power, for example, are the bases for the frames of reference that socialization researchers choose to explain political phenomena.

The frame, or set, has relationship to what the social scientist will investigate and conclude. Of course, epistemological choices also represent a choice of sets, as do ontological choices. What is the basis of the choice? Is this ultimately objective? Of great importance are those elements which are not specific by the set or network, those phenomena which lurk about, not susceptible to discovery because discovery and validation are indivisibly connected, and something will always remain outside of that set.[20] Nonrationality and uncertainty, thus, become represented as anomalies in our most systematic attempts to describe social and political phenomena in terms of theory—particularly that variety of theory denoted as behavioral theory—and become representative of the unconscious elements or projections involved in personal interactions. Indeed certain obvious qualities of human existence cannot be behaviorally or scientifically explored, and are therefore in actuality ignored, simply because they are not open to rational empirical investigation, or to rational philosophical inquiry in the traditional sense, within the dominant knowledge structure of the discipline within which the scholar works. As Wrong notes, the oversocialized concept of human nature ignores both the "beast and the angel" in humans. Wrong is right.

Political Inquiry and Human Nature

The rationalist view of human nature neglects the extent to which people seek authentic answers to questions which transcend historical and political situations, answers to questions which are, at once, personal and universal. These kinds of questions are not subject to cumulatively more highly defined answers through behavioral or rational research since they are bound to remain problematic and therefore uncertain. Jung states it clearly:

> We cannot directly explore the unconscious psyche because the unconscious is just unconscious, and we have therefore no relation to it. We can only deal with the conscious products which we suppose have originated in the field called the unconscious. . . . Whatever we have to say about the unconscious is what the conscious mind says about it. . . . Consciousness is like a surface of a skin upon a vast unconscious area of unknown extent. We do not know how far the unconscious rules because we simply know nothing of it. You cannot say anything about a thing of which you know nothing. When we say "the unconscious" we often mean to convey something by the term, but as a matter of fact we simply convey that we do not know what the unconscious is.[21]

11

The failure to see the unknown of which Jung speaks condemns social scientists to studying the human fossil rather than the human being. The social scientist has been placed under abstract arrest, having paradoxically jailed himself much like Kafka's Joseph K.

A social scientist provides the order in what appears to be an uncertain and unintelligible world, to "obtain organized knowledge of social reality."[22]   Max Weber saw this.

> Order is brought into this chaos only on the condition that in every case only a part of concrete reality is interesting and significant to us, because only it is related to the cultural values with which we approach reality.[23]

The order "out there" is the order of our conceptual screens laid over reality.   Certainly subjectivity is involved in choice of one's cultural values, but additionally it must be seen that the psyche can never be merely socially constituted.   The unconscious cannot be "explained away" in such terms.   Perhaps the most frightful discovery made by a rationalistic social scientist is that the nonrational is also real.   Nonetheless, Weber's analysis may be applied to some extent and he certainly provides insight as to rationalized contexts.   A social scientist is, of course, raised within a given culture and linguistic structure; trained within institutions as to appropriate roles and statuses, including what will pass for knowledge; and, finally, is involved in the legitimation of his or her work.   All of these factors, of course, bear upon the interpretive faculties of the social scientist.[23]   Thus, the social scientist is always a part of what he or she studies in this sense and can never be a fish out of the water.[25]   Often, then, attention is focused upon questions which the social scientist has accepted as significant, thus ignoring other questions, other possibilities.   The discipline will define the means of "seeing" historical situations, with inevitable questions and answers.   The tautological problem here is that the discipline also defines the rules of evidence.   What will pass for acceptable evidence becomes crucial of course.   Goldberg notes that:

> The set of constraints which enable one to characterize a field of inquiry as a "discipline" deal very much with the question of what shall count as persuasive evidence.[26]

Answers become merely variations of an already prevalent schematization, but are disguised as novel from time to time while, in fact, their function appears to be defensive.   Voegelin observes that:

> The experience of resistance, of possible or actual defeat now, is the occasion on which the meaning of truth comes into clearer view.   In so far as the order of society does not exist automatically but must be

founded, preserved, and defended, those who are on the side of order represent the truth, while their enemies represent disorder and falsehood.[27]

It is not unusual for the rationalistic social scientist, on the side of order, to ignore the nonrational "disorder and falsehood." Such ignorance is a syndrome which provides the bulkheading of the doctrinaire rationalist view.

The characteristics of the human psyche bear directly upon the question of inquiry in the social sciences. Pressing the analysis further, Severyn Bruyn argues that political and social reality does not exist absolutely, but that the discriminating mind also translates the world through its networks, thus giving structure and meaning to an apparently external world.

What becomes known to the mind as a "phenomenon" is that which is perceived, which is in turn the result of constructive activity of the mind. The form of that activity is contained "a priori" in the structure of the intellect, and it imposes a certain order and meaning upon what is to be given to the senses from the outside world.[28]

What Bruyn has chosen to call the "constructive activity" of the mind, is quite similar to Owen Barfield's notion of "figuration."

When a lady complained to Whistler that she did not see the world he painted, he is said to have replied: "No, ma'am, but don't you wish you could?" Both Whistler and the lady were really referring to that activity— which in Whistler's case was intenser than the lady's. Ought it be called a "mental" activity? For, as the organs of sense are required to convert the unrepresented into sensations for us, so something is required in us to convert sensations into "things." It is this something that I mean. And it will avoid confusion if I purposely choose an unfamiliar and little-used word and call it, at the risk of infelicity, figuration.[29]

It would seem, then, that rationalist inquiry is, in essence, tautological. An elaborate symbolic universe reinforces the prevailing knowledge structure, is always changing form, and maintains the fantasy of truth, aided by the ignorance of the ordering activity of one's own cognitive processes. Lest this essay fall into pessimism, it may be hoped that as Hannah Arendt has said,

True understanding does not tire of interminable dialogue and "vicious circles" because it trusts that imagination will eventually catch at least a glimpse of the always frightening light of truth.[30]

13

While truth may seem frightening, rational models of human nature, however, have not appropriately addressed imagination or intuition as such, most likely because they cannot. Again, it must be stressed that this does not mean that rational inquiry should not proceed, but rather that it must not take itself so seriously since it barely touches the human condition. Historical images of human nature, particularly those positive models, assumed human rationality and perfectability, then connected these assumptions to liberal democratic thinking in contrast to conservative thought which did not rely on the rational capacities of people as positive, and thus fell directly upon authority, tradition, and the leader to maintain and support order. The avoidance of uncertainty can be seen, for example, in the writings of Locke; reflection was a concept in relation to which rationality was actually extraneous. And so it was within the school of British empiricism, where similar "abstractions" to account for rationality were found in Bentham's enlightened self-interest and, of course, in the amusing concept of Adam Smith's invisible hand. Are these truly rational?

Early behavioralism was also an expression of the irrationally rational image. Behavioralists responded to an extreme to the positing of instincts, drives, and motivations by the psychoanalytic schools. They claimed no knowledge whatsoever about what went on inside the human being--to maintain "objectivity," the human being became vacuous, a black box, a set of behaviors--which was, of course, an assumption of questionable rational status. The emphasis of objectivity led to the measuring of stimuli and the observing of responses--much like an input-output model with increasing reliance on a positivist methodology which had seemed so successful in the natural sciences. Although contemporary behavioralists have claimed to have gone beyond this initial conceptualization, the basic frame of reference remains the same, only the arcane means of manipulating data have changed. The result of developing more sophisticated statistical techniques has been simply to mire the dialogue at that level while ignoring substantive questions regarding human nature. The reason is due here, not to the subject of study, but to, as Thorson argues, "science, in order to make the procedures and the conclusions more scientific."[31] To speak of a total human being, of the psyche, or even of the imagery of mental events, given the behaviorist set of reference, becomes undesirable since inner life is itself unobservable.[32] Therefore, to meet the demands of the methodology, the human being is assumed by behavioralists to be similar to a computer, governed by certain rules, which processes stimuli or sense data and magically transmutes them into responses.

Jung was quite aware of the danger involved in the use of highly rationalized scientific and mathematized knowledge and language in describing psychic content, and felt that such usage was, in fact less accurate than other ways of speaking to the problem. Jung said that,

> I deliberately and consciously give preference to a
> dramatic, mythological way of thinking and speaking,
> because this is not only more expressive but also more

14

exact that an abstract scientific terminology, which is
want to toy with the notion that its theoretic formulations may one fine day be resolved into algebra
equations.[33]

He has directed our attention to the problematics and uncertainty of
abstraction in constructing models of human behavior based on experience:

> Any theory based on experience is necessarily statis-
> tical; that is to say, it formulates an ideal average
> which abolishes all exceptions at either end of the scale
> and replaces them by an abstract mean. This mean is
> quite valid, though it need not necessarily occur in
> reality.[34]

Rational theory, in this sense, becomes less accurate in terms of
understanding individual facts as it attempts to assert universal validity.
This is not a problem except, as Jung points out, that the character of
reality is predominantly that of "irregularity." That is, "while reflecting
an indisputable aspect of reality, it can falsify the actual truth in a most
misleading way."[35]

Garfinkel is in concurrence with Jung on this point and argues that
social scientific models of human beings show human beings as "judg-
mental dopes." This problem occurs through standardization of common
understandings. In short, the patterns of behavior relate far more to the
models employed by the social scientist than to the empirical realities of
people being studied. This is a self-maintaining illusion of certainty in
which the actuality of standardization is utilized to conceptualize the
nature and effects of human phenomena that conform to standardized
expectancies. Garfinkel states:

> Many studies have documented the finding that the
> social standardization of common understandings, irre-
> spective of what it is that is standardized, orients
> persons' actions to scenic events, and furnishes persons
> the grounds upon which departures from perceivedly
> normal courses of affairs are detectable, restoration is
> made, and effortful action is mobilized.

> Generally they [social scientists] have acknowledged but
> otherwise neglected the fact that by these same actions
> persons discover, create and sustain this standardiza-
> tion. An important and prevalent consequence of this
> neglect is that of being misled about the nature and
> conditions of stable actions. This occurs by making out
> the member of society to be a judgmental dope. . . .[36]

While Garfinkel's language may be ponderous, his point should not be
overlooked. He is drawing notice to the observation that the individual

15

as such is disregarded as merely a unit and that the social scientific solution to this methodological ignorance, in which the individual is actually considered to be epiphenomenal, is

> to portray what the member's actions will have come to by using the stable structures—i.e., what they came to—as a point of theoretical departure from which to portray the necessary character of the pathways whereby the end result is assembled. Hierarchies of need dispositions, and common culture as enforced rules or action, are favored devices for bringing the problem of necessary inference to terms, although at the cost of making out the person-in-society to be a judgmental dope.[37]

In this sense we learn nothing, but are apparently willing to engage in all sorts of fantastic stories about human nature. That is, we learn that people are pokable; susceptible to stimuli and orient themselves acordingly (or reject them); but we do not learn what meaning individuals attach to their responses to the stimuli, for example, since they may just appear to be pokable.

Social scientists modify what they study, they are participants in their researches, and this fundamental characteristic of doing research cannot be merely disregarded. All of this has not been to say, on the other hand, that researches into human nature should be rejected or abandoned. Quite the contrary. One's empirical wits should be kept keen. However, social scientists must be aware of what their researching means. Perspective ought to be present.

Seen in another manner, subject and object are complementary, as well as rational and nonrational, for one could not be "human" except for other people, language, and the social and psychological learning involved in the unfolding and illumination of everyday life. This is quite different, again, than the notion that a person is completely molded by the norms and values of their culture or their physiology. The psyche is a continually unfolding potentiality and is, therefore, a vital paradox. This is a view quite different from the magical problems of "identity" or "personality" which prevail within the rational social sciences. To be concerned with a depth view of human phenomena, the rational and the non-rational, the unconscious as well as the conscious sources of human activity require exploration. This essay will explore the unconscious fear of death, Phobos, and its relation to the problems raised above, for the issues raised in this chapter are, of course, not as simple as they have been put. This exploration, in turn, requires a reconceptualization of the human self usually found in the social science literature which, then, requires a different kind of thinking, a thinking which values metaphor and symbol as well as empiricism and rationality. Of considerable importance is the problem of unconsciousness and its relation to consciousness. That is the main point—the unconscious, or unknown and therefore uncertain, sources of human activity. How can these be represented? To answer this question the essay will turn to an explication of Jung's model of the self, or psyche, and an acknowledgment that the actual face of human nature may consist of nothing but exceptions to the rule--that many things exist autonomously of our understanding, and that their existence is not contingent upon rational or empirical verification.

The psyche is, in short, a symbol for the place of experience. As a totality symbol it also represents what is uncertain, unknown, or incomprehensible in terms of ego-consciousness. The greatest unknown is death, of course, and the fear of death provides the drive to rigidly cling to the abstract order of rational theories or the political order of the state in alienated or authoritarian forms. Before coming to the explication of alienation, authoritarianism, and the consequent failure of participation, a discussion of the pertinent aspects of Jung's psychology and the unconscious is necessary and will, hopefully, assist in the suspension of the polarized view described here and provide some clarity regarding the immortalizing drive underlying the attempts to rationalize human nature. The illusion of rational certainty simply cannot be sustained when it is sincerely and critically examined in depth. Jung's great respect for the unknown and unknowable and his consequent understanding of the impossibility of a complete description of human nature, in rational terms, is incorporated into his psychology. This is why I find Jung so significant to my own theory. Jung's symbolic psychology presents a more accurate picture, broadly speaking, than the rational view which tends to ignore the unknown, the unconscious for the fear of nothingness. The rational view, kept in perspective, can assist our study, but taken uncritically, the inflated rational view merely creates a social science without tears or laughter; this amounts to a loss of perspective with serious implications for the study of human activity.

Notes for Chapter I

[1]C. G. Jung, Two Essays on Analytical Psychology, 2d ed. (Princeton: Princeton University Press, 1966), p. 119.

[2]C. G. Jung, Aion, 2d ed., Bollingen Series XX, Collected Works, vol. 9, pt. 2 (Princeton: Princeton University Press, 1968), p. 5, emphasis mine.

[3]See: Jacques Ellul, The Technological Society (New York: Alfred A. Knopf, 1964). Ellul's analysis of technique in the human sciences is useful here.

[4]Jung, Two Essays on Analytical Psychology, p. 177, emphasis mine.

[5]C. G. Jung, Psychological Types, Bollingen Series XX, Collected Works, vol. 6 (Princeton: Princeton University Press, 1971), p. 73.

[6]See: Dennis H. Wrong, "The Oversocialized Conception of Man in Modern Sociology," American Sociological Review 26 (April 1961):183-193. Wrong lucidly elaborates these two assumptions in the socialization literature and has provided several ideas for this section.

[7]Clyde Kluckhohn, Mirror for Man (New York: Whittlesey House, 1949), p. 197.

[8]F. Elkin, The Child and Society: The Process of Socialization (New York: Random House, 1960), p. 4.

[9]D. F. Aberle, "Culture and Socialization," in F. L. K. Hsu, ed., Psychological Anthropology: Approaches to Culture and Personality (Homewood, Ill.: Dorsey Press, 1961), p. 387. Also see: Melvin L. DeFleur et al., Sociology: Human Society (Glenview, Ill.: Scott, Foresman & Co., 1973).

[10]David Easton and Jack Dennis, Children in the Political System (New York: McGraw-Hill, 1969), p. 4.

[11]Roger Brown, Social Psychology (New York: Free Press, 1965), p. 350.

[12]Sigmund Freud, Civilization and Its Discontents (New York: W. W. Norton, 1957), p. 114.

[13]Lewis A. Froman, Jr., "Learning Political Attitudes," Western Political Quarterly 15 (June 1962):305.

[14]C. G. Jung, The Structure and Dynamics of the Psyche, 2d ed., Bollingen Series XX, Collected Works, vol. 8 (Princeton: Princeton University Press, 1968), pp. 325-326.

[15]Wrong, p. 188.

[16]DeFleur et al., Sociology: Human Society, p. 153.

[17]Ralph Linton, The Cultural Background of Personality (New York: Appleton-Century Co, 1945), p. 91.

[18]See: Albert Bandura and Richard Walters, Social Learning and Personality Development (New York: Holt, Rinehart & Winston, 1963); and Neal Miller and John Dollard, Social Learning and Imitation (New Haven: Yale University Press, 1941).

[19]See: Norman Frohlich and Joe A. Oppenheimer, "Governmental Violence and Tax Revenue," in Herbert Hirsch and David Perry, eds., Violence as Politics (New York: Harper & Row, 1973), pp. 72-88; and Anthony Downs, An Economic Theory of Democracy (New York: Harper & Row, 1957).

[20]The frame or set is always teleological because classification is itself purposeful. The problem is raised when a person is asked to define something. An insightful response to such a request would be to ask for a definition of "define," which would again demonstrate the problematics of abstraction. An example of this problem is the implicit assumption with regard to control found in most social and political theory. The order or the need for order (adaptation-control) that is found in "the world" or in "the individual" is the character of the theory, in this case, not of the world itself, although it seems clear that people can be conditioned to fit the theory.

[21]C. G. Jung, Analytical Psychology: Its Theory and Practice (New York: Vintage Books, 1968), pp. 6-7.

[22]Alfred Schutz, "Concept and Theory Formation in the Social Sciences," in Maurice A. Natanson, ed., Philosophy of the Social Sciences: A Reader (New York: Random House, 1963), p. 236.

[23]Max Weber, "Objectivity in the Social Sciences," in May Brodbeck, ed., Readings in the Philosophy of the Social Sciences (New York: Macmillan, 1968), p. 90.

[24]See: Peter L. Berger and Thomas Luckmann, The Social Construction of Reality (New York: Anchor Books, 1967).

[25]The defense to this observation is the claim to objectivity, a claim that is often made in bad faith, so it would seem, since absolute objectivity and absolute subjectivity must meet. Only arbitrariness

19

preserves the illusion of the dichotomy and the claim to objectivity as Truth.

[26]Arthur S. Goldberg, "On the Need for Contextualist Criteria: A Reply to Professor Gunnell," American Political Science Review 63 (December 1969):54-55.

[27]Voegelin, The New Science of Politics (Chicago: University of Chicago Press, 1952), pp. 54-55.

[28]Severyn Bruyn, The Human Perspective in Sociology: The Methodology of Participant Observation (Englewood Cliffs, N.J.: Prentice-Hall, 1966), p. 96.

[29]Owen Barfield, Saving the Appearances: A Study in Idolatry (New York: Harcourt, Brace & World, n.d.), p. 24.

[30]Hannah Arendt, "Understanding and Politics," Partisan Review 20 (July-August 1953):392.

[31]Thomson L. Thorson, Biopolitics (New York: Holt, Rinehart & Winston, 1970), p. 46.

[32]Abraham Maslow commented, with regard to this problem, that, "If the only tool you have is a hammer, you tend to treat everything as if it were a nail." (Abraham Maslow, The Psychology of Science: A Reconnaissance [Chicago: Henry Regnery, 1969].) If one's tool is a certain methodology, or say, a computer, people will surely become the nails appropriate to the methodology or technology being utilized. William James spoke to the problem of this sort of teleology inquiry when he noted that, "Every way of classifying a thing is but a way of handling it for some particular purpose." (William James, "The Sentiment of Rationality," in Essays in Pragmatism [New York: Scribners, 1948], p. 148.) It would seem fruitful to be conscious of this in analyzing the human self or the world in rational and technical ways.

[33]Jung, Aion, p. 13. One might add that toying with differential or integral calculus is only a more sophisticated form of gnostic hocus-pocus than algebra when one applies it to human beings. Arnold J. Toynbee came to the same conclusion when he found rationalist explanations to be useless. Toynbee wrote: "The breakdown of these . . . drove me to turn to mythology. I took this turning rather self-consciously and shame-facedly, as though it were a provocatively retrograde step. I might have been less diffident . . . if I had been acquainted at the time with the works of C. G. Jung, they would have given me the clue." (Arnold J. Toynbee, Civilization on Trial [New York: Oxford University Press, 1948], p. 11.)

[34]C. G. Jung, The Undiscovered Self (New York: New American Library, 1958), p. 16.

[35]Ibid., p. 17.

[36]Harold Garfinkle, Studies in Ethnomethodology (Englewood Cliffs, N.J.: Prentice-Hall, 1967), pp. 66-67, emphasis mine.

[37]Ibid., p. 68.

CHAPTER II

PSYCHE AND THE ILLUSION OF CAUSALITY

History is a pattern of timeless moments.
- T. S. Eliot[1]

The paradox of society is that, on the one hand, the idea is given that the psyche is bounded by one's skin and that it acts on its own, as an independent agent, separately from the society or nonrationality—so that, society appears to confer independence--yet, on the other hand, one is defined as an independent agent only in order to be held accountable to society for "one's" action. The nature of the situation is then akin to being "half-free," for the person must not be so independent as not to yield to the rules which give him the definition. In other words, independence is given and taken away simultaneously, but the contradiction remains implicit--the secret is not revealed. Psychologically, the situation is a double-bind. The theory of causality itself is a fundamental double-bind underlying the loss of perspective problem discussed in the last chapter. Therefore, it is causality which will occupy attention in this chapter.

Causality, Time, and Space

Causality presents one with the double-bind problem, for it seems impossible to live in the world unless one accepts causality, yet it is impossible to understand the nature of the psyche or human nature when causality is uncritically accepted. The rationalistic vision tends to be dependent upon causality or its variant—probability.

To elaborate, the acceptance of causality is the granting of the independent and simultaneous existence of individual objects, any one of which may be acted upon by another—yet, this is the impossibility. To begin, the principle, so to speak, in the discrimination and objectivation of consciousness is thought. It is objectified by what is not stated or cognized, because for consciousness to appear to be objectified, an independent agent is necessary.

The problem of cause and effect is a key to the empirical method, a point of view which has been overemphasized in the social sciences of our time despite serious evidence of shortcomings. Quite often when a phenomenon occurs where the cause is unknown, it will simply be concluded that the cause is, for now, beyond acquisition since to admit to no causes is unacceptable for, according to the rationalist idea, the "natural laws" governing human nature are "out there" to be discovered.

There is another vision, however, that one may take with regard to cause and effect, in terms of the social sciences, and that is that cause and effect are, in reality, the same thing viewed from different perspectives. This is the paradoxical perspective and may prove more fruitful in understanding human behavior. That is, the effect is always potential in the cause, and the cause is always potential in the effect. It is only the posited existence of a cause which allows an effect to be noticed. But it does not end here.

The notion of causality can, of course, be pointed back to the extramundane through the asking of the following, not often asked, question: "What is the scientific and empirical foundation of causation itself?" This question is not usually put because the doctrinaire view of cause and effect excludes uncertainty-provoking questions about the ground of existence. Those questions, in the thinking of many social scientists, generally belong to the philosophers. In the case of causation, it is just as well, I suppose, since there appears to be no proof for it; the character armor of social science, at bottom, rests upon faith, and, therefore, must be defended by the faithful. Causation is merely a premise, neither a fixed part of one's ego-consciousness nor a fixed part of the world. All such axiomatic notions, like causality, are notions of convenience, are powerful means of organizing knowledge; in exaggerated form they are defenses, constructed to a purpose. This means that the theory of causality is teleological in nature when examined in depth. This again, is not easily admitted by one overly committed to the empirical perspective because this view would seem destructive of empirical science. The great irony is that in actuality the reverse is true--inasmuch as social scientists unconsciously participate in the doctrine of causality, as it applies to human nature, they take part in the destruction of science by denying the transpersonal which is quite real but which cannot be caught by the empirical net.

Of course, arguments have been addressed to the problem of causality that has been raised here. Among these are those based in the principles of probability theory. This is another convenience which seemingly permits social scientists to speak of probable cause, to speak of various types of errors which are presumed to be attributable to imprecise measurement, imprecise theory, or imprecise technique when, in fact, reality itself is imprecise. Reality is made precise with the use of statistical techniques by ignoring its imprecision. The rationalist school recoils from speculations about the ground of existence, which underlie its own work because the problematics of inquiry in this sense bring the ego-inflated mind to a standstill. A believing empiricist, the person with a polarized vision, simply could not do his or her work and consider such questions at the same time even though such questions point to realities of human experience and are crucial if human nature is to be more wholly understood.

In describing human nature, a social scientist will normally be articulating processes and structures. Processes, however, cannot be described without describing the structure of space and time within which

24

they occur. Similarly, when social scientists describe the world as comprehensively as they are able, they are specifying the form of the human being, because the scientific account of the world is actually an account of experiments, of what individuals do as they explore the world. From the other view, when the form of the human being is comprehensively described—physical characteristics, language, political behavior, and activity—the social scientist is describing the world. Separation of them cannot occur, unless, of course, one does not look very deeply. What, then, may be said of time and space?

Time, like space, cannot be conceived of apart from the objects it is supposed to permeate. Time is no more than a conception and is never immediately experienced. A present time is only the individual's manner of delineating a certain collection of thought which has just now been present in consciousness. Modern physics, unlike the social sciences, has been aware of this.[2] All of this is not to say that our frameworks, networks, systems of reference, language forms and so forth are somehow in error, but, simply, where over-emphasized, they cannot express that which is implicit in them, and, above all, they can never express the entirety. This is, of course, a briefly stated analysis of the major obstacle of the social sciences in addressing human nature. In "The Theory of Psychoanalysis," Jung comments:

> We must never forget that the world is, in the first
> place, a subjective phenomenon. The impressions we
> receive from those accidental happenings are also our
> own doing.[3]

It is quite important to understand that the "world" is, in the phenomenal sense, made up of time, space, and causality. Yet, these are but abstractions from reality. Time, space, and causality are representations of reality, not reality itself. Jung, articulating his formulation of synchronicity, in what amounts to a seemingly radical perspective, says that time and space are nothing other than reified concepts. The implication of this understanding is enormous to say the least.

> In themselves, space and time consist of nothing. They
> are hypostatized concepts born of the discriminating
> mind. . . . They are . . . essentially psychic in origin.
> . . . But if space and time are only apparently
> properties of bodies in motion and are created by the
> intellectual needs of the observer, then relativization by
> psychic conditions is no longer a matter for astonish-
> ment.[4]

If time and space, in themselves, consist of nothing, then causality, as such, likewise consists of nothing. Our notions of time, space, and causality are reifications of what is essentially psychic. In fact, despite our efforts in terms of rationalism to predict, and order, the future remains unknown and uncertain—it remains unconscious. Future events simply cannot be spatially present. It is not possible to actually choose ends.[5] However, the unknown seems to be feared and, in turn, drives us to our stories about who we are and where we are and where we will be. In this undisciplined manner, social science has participated in the destruction of science through its rational-control bias, which is at best consoling, but not particularly constructive.

Jung and Acausality

It is somewhat difficult to explicate Jung's idea of an acausal connecting principle--synchronicity--without having understood his general approach. Jung makes a statement, however, which is a good starting point for a discussion of synchronicity:

> . . . we are not entitled to conclude from the apparent space-time quality of our perception that there is no form of existence without space and time.[6]

Time, space, and causality are ideas created in the differentiating activity of thoughts, of the intellectual function of the psyche. It is usually clear to a person, for example, that if he or she examined their physical body now, for example, that the body has changed. Similarly, an examination of beliefs, opinions, thoughts, and so forth as a child and then as an older person, or even from moment to moment, would indicate a similar change. That is, mind and body have always changed for all of us--along with, one might add, the world. Where, then, is the changeless referent that allows one to notice changes in mind and body? It must lie outside mind/body. The reflecting psyche, therefore, also lies outside of time and space. Now, in this case, can one use causality, which is composed of time and space, to understand human nature which is beyond time and space? The point is, put simply, that one can account for change only within the context created by time and space assumptions. Any empirical referent has time and space qualities. An empirical referent rests on assumptions about time and space. The self-reflective activity of the human psyche is beyond this. It is immediate and real to us all however. It is not hypothetical even though it is beyond time and space, and causality. It is immediate and non-changing. It cannot be fully analyzed empirically. Yet, change always occurs in the nonchanging immediacy and reality of the psyche. Objects appear and objects disappear. The psyche remains. Reification problems arise only when one is identified with the objects of awareness. Then, if one wishes to empirically "see" change, one must make the dubious assumption that the object in relation to which change is to be noticed will not change itself. Jung comments further on the perseverance of the psyche:

> The nature of the psyche reaches into obscurities far beyond the scope of our understanding. It contains as many riddles as the universe with its galactic systems, before whose majestic configurations only a mind lacking in imagination can fail to admit its own insufficiency. This extreme uncertainty of human

comprehension makes the intellectualistic hubbub not only ridiculous, but also deplorably dull. . . . One of the most fatal of the sociological and psychological errors which in our time is so fruitful is the supposition that something can become entirely different all in a moment. . . . Restlessness begets meaninglessness, and the lack of meaning in life is a soul-sickness whose full extent and full import our age has not yet begun to comprehend.[7]

Failure to understand the deep and transcendent nature of the human psyche and instead to accept wholly empirical or rational models or substitutes for the human self, is to become acquainted with meaninglessness and is a celebration of death in its subtle dimension. It is in this manner that our contemporary society can be characterized as gnostic, and this is why "isms" of political and religious nature have flourished and will likely continue to do so. The social sciences are possessed by their own isms and thus tend to imitate the general problem rather than explain or understand it.

Causality supports the frame of reference of statistical laws; of ideal averages. A more refined mathematics is not the solution, for the language of the psyche is not mathematical, it is metaphorical. Resort to theories of probability is merely a resort to probable cause. That is, causality is inferred from the macrophysical. It is, however, difficult to assume causality in the individual case, since the individual is, in a sense, an exception to any descriptive theory which must necessarily deal with ideal averages, thereby eliminating the exception. Jung became interested in the notion of synchronicity as a means of discussing events which were connected, but not causally connected. On the other hand, inquiry within the social sciences aims at regularities, certainties, or patterns—events which seem to be repeated and causally connected. Since this sort of analysis is essentially descriptive, and therefore ultimately statistical in character, unique or exceptional phenomena are not included. A research design carried out by a social scientist is, likewise, intended to give answers to questions previously conceptualized by the social scientist. The problem here, as Jung sees it, is that:

Absolutely unique and ephemeral events whose existence we have no means of either denying or proving can never be the object of empirical science. . . . The so called possibility of such events is of no importance whatever, for the criterion of what is possible in any age is derived from the age's rationalistic assumptions. There are no "absolute" natural laws to whose authority one can appeal in support of one's prejudices.[8]

So, we seem to be left with arbitrarily declaring that relationships between variables exist if our rationalistic theories acquire consensual status, if the tenets of probability theory are met, and if our statistical techniques obtain. However, this still does not truly explain the psyche.

In fact, the more precise empirical notions of human nature become, the less important are the questions addressed.

Synchronicity is a notion which Jung hopes is more congenial to understanding the psyche. Synchronicity is a kind of meaningful coincidence. Jung argues that there are events which seem to be linked, but which are noncausal in nature. Events which are related by "meaningful cross-connection."[9] Synchronicity is Jung's hypothesis of an explanatory element for events which cannot be considered to be causally related and he regards synchronicity as "a psychically conditioned relativity of space and time."[10] That is, he recognizes, in relation to the psyche that:

> Space and time are, so to speak, "elastic" and can apparently be reduced almost to vanishing point, as though they were dependent on psychic conditions and did not exist in themselves but were only "postulated" by the conscious mind. In man's original view of the world, as we find it among primitives, space and time have a very precarious existence. They become "fixed" concepts only in the course of his mental development, thanks largely to the introduction of measurement.[11]

Jung goes on to maintain that these symbolic parallels rest upon the archetypal bases of what he has called the collective unconscious. This will be examined in the following chapter.

Jung does not mean that synchronicity is just the simultaneous occurrence of two episodes. This sort of occurrence he has referred to as "synchronism." In distinction to this notion, synchronicity is the "coincidence in time of two or more causally unrelated events which have the same or similar meaning."[12] Synchronicity is psychic in character, and is associated with the archetypal contents of the collective unconscious. Jung simply describes archetypes as the

> . . . formal factors responsible for the organization of unconscious psychic processes: they are "patterns of behavior." At the same time they have a "specific charge" and develop numinous effects which express themselves as affects.[13]

Synchronicity can be characterized, then, as being psychically associated with a particular state in which several episodes seemingly occurring outside the psyche are possessed of the same or similar meaning. Jung goes on to state that "synchronistic events rest on the simultaneous occurrence of two different psychic states.[14] Since time and space, as normally experienced, are suspended in this sense, even future predictions, not casually derivable, are

> synchronistic, since they are experienced as psychic images in the present, as though the objective event

28

already existed. An unexpected content which is directly or indirectly connected with the ordinary psychic state: this is what I call synchronicity, and I maintain that we are dealing with exactly the same category of events whether their objectivity appears separated from my consciousness in space or in time.[15]

Synchronicity is not temporal or spatial in nature, and is, thus, noncausal as well. It must be recalled that time, space, and causality are, on the other hand, of the psychic mode of intellection, and do not exist apart from that function. Jung states:

Since experience has shown that under certain conditions space and time can be reduced almost to zero, causality disappears along with them, because causality is bound up with the existence of space and time and physical changes, and consists essentially in the succession of cause and effect. For this reason synchronistic phenomena cannot in principle be associated with any conceptions of causality. Hence the interconnection of meaningfully coincident factors must necessarily be thought of as acausal.[16]

In terms of synchronicity, Jung is attempting an exegesis of phenomena for which empirical science has provided no adequate explanation. This does not mean we must dismiss causality. Synchronicity, as a phenomenal explication, is a complement to causality and may take the form of a concurrence or correspondence of internal perceptions with the past, present, or future external occurrences. Although Jung postulated synchronicity as a formal factor, it nonetheless discloses the meaningful aspect of phenomena beyond the reaches of logic, rationality and empiricism. Of course, the perspective of wholeness in relation to meaning and knowledge is one of Jung's purposes. To take an extreme attitude toward either subjectivity or objectivity was to render an aspect of consciousness unconscious with the consequent disordering of the individual. Instead, Jung felt that one must keep both views, understanding and knowledge, in sight at once even though they appear to be contradictory. The apparent conflict between the two, states Jung, "cannot be solved by an either-or but only by a kind of two-way thinking."[17] Understanding requires an unfettered openness in all directions, whereas rationalistic knowledge "presupposes all sorts of knowledge about mankind in general."[18] Thus it must also be remembered that this essay does not advocate abolishing our empirical wits, but rather that empirical knowledge should not lose sight of its complement.

The symbolic nature of Jung's exegesis of the psyche must be continually kept in mind. To fail to do so is to not only fail to understand Jung, but also to reduce the meaning of his work to mere logic and rationalisms. Given the highly rational-material basis of our own society, meaning itself has become doctrinaire and rationalistic, thus ironically providing the ultimate justification for the State in which case the transcendent ground of existence, the only basis for psychic organization in the individual, is lost in degraded and convoluted terms which no longer refer to psychic reality, but only to ideologically-based second-order or reified expressions. The problem under discussion is a problem of society in general as well. Social scientists tend to participate in that problem. In so far as collective tendencies remain unconscious through the polarized social scientific claim to objectivity and causality, social science is, so to speak, possessed of the very demons it seeks to explain. Mass man lives within all of us, including social scientists. Jung attempts to illuminate this. And so instead of the notion of causality and probable causality which still prevail in the social sciences, Jung approaches the inadequacy of the notion of causality, probability, and determinacy in understanding human nature, by explicitly introducing the principle of synchronicity in contradistinction to the causal implications of empirical science. Jung, in fact, maintained:

> A science can never be a Weltanschauung, but merely the tool with which to make one . . . no one is without a Weltanschauung of some sort. Even in the extreme case, he will at least have the Weltanschauung that education and environment have forced upon him.[19]

When the problem of human nature, existence, and consequent human activity is investigated, and inasmuch as our speculation is to be considered scientific, it must be tempered by the reality that:

> Science is not the summa of life, . . . it is actually only one of the psychological attitudes, only one of the forms of human thought.[20]

Because of its power, however, causality has a seductive nature and scholars and philosophers have been logically speculating about the causes of the world, the origins of culture, and the genesis of personality beyond the reach of memory, probing and searching as to the place, the time, and the manner of its commencement. But, questions about origination can also be shown to be completely illogical, thus again revealing the unconscious--the unknown.[21] For example, if the world, or culture, or behavior, or personality, had its inception at any point in space, or if it were the effect of some cause, then space already existed and causality already existed. The questions are metaphysically illogical and they make no sense simply because time, space and causality cannot be defined or explained in terms of time, space and causality except tautologically. The line is really a circle. Progress is a pattern of "timeless moments." Models of human nature or the self which fail to recognize this point bear, in turn, only a poverty-stricken relation to the psyche, but insofar as they are believed, they provide the illusion of certainty. The object perceived can never be really separated from the subject which permeates it. All of our certainties are also subjective.

Ego-consciousness is based largely on the physical senses. Stating this in other terms, the field of vision, which is taken to be external to

30

the individual, is, in fact, inside the person, the subject. That specific state of the nervous system, a state which for that instant is a constituent element of the person, is seeing. In like manner, a sound is not, strictly speaking, heard by a person. The sound is the hearing, removed from hearing it is nothing more than a vibration in the air. For example, Jung states:

> If . . . you look at our physical world and if you compare what our consciousness makes of this same world, you find all sorts of mental pictures which do not exist as objective facts. For instance, we see colour and hear sound, but in reality they are oscillations. As a matter of fact, we need a laboratory with very complicated apparatus in order to establish a picture of that world apart from our senses and apart from our psyche; and I suppose it is very much the same with our unconscious--we ought to have a laboratory in which we could establish by objective methods how things really are when in an unconscious condition. So any conclusion or any statement I make in the course of my lectures about the unconscious should be taken with that critique in mind. It is always as if, and you should never forget that restriction.[22]

Of course, the world is more certain, more likely to appear as immortal if the as if remains implicit. Stated in its simplest terms, perception is a field relationship; that is, between what is often referred to as a sense-datum and its corresponding sense organ, there exists an immediate and inseparable connection. Jung makes the same point with regard to unconsciousness and the psyche.

The notion that sensations are caused by stimuli external to the senses, to be repetitive, is illusory. One could imagine what the world might be like if, instead of possessing the five senses, one only possessed four, and had, for example, absolutely no sense of touch. The world, under this condition, could not possibly be the world whose "real" existence is to be so taken for granted.

The Unconscious Factor and the Task of Social Science

One of the manners in which the problematics of the rationalistic models of human nature are "resolved" is in the attempt to reduce human nature to the physical, to chemistry, to genetics, and so forth. This is curious since there is no actual distinction to be made between the mental and the physical despite the rational nature-nurture arguments which have been carried on between scholars who focus rationally on the social aspects of human beings and scholars who focus rationally on the biological aspects of human beings and the "compromisers" who focus rationally on the sociobiology of human beings. The physical, however, attracts a certain number of scholars because, it would seem, the physical

31

appears to be more susceptible to a scientific-like methodology. Metaphysical considerations, of course, from this point of view, are regarded as annoyances not deserving of attention, or inclusion, but rather as wastes of time--if it cannot be "tested," then a work can be dismissed as inadequate or ambiguous as it poses metaphysical questions rather than being grounded in the practical scientific enterprise. Yet rationalistic scholarship often passes as real, practical, and scientific even though it too is essentially speculative. Jung elaborates this view:

> However indignant people may get about "metaphysical" phantoms: when cell processes are explained vitalistically, they nevertheless continue to regard the physical hypothesis as "scientific," although it is no less fantastic. But it fits with the materialistic prejudice, and that it turns the psychic into the physical, becomes scientifically sacrosanct.[23]

Similarly, organism/environment is a unified phenomenon, although the social scientific view sustains the rational dichotomy then posits causality to reunite them. The basis for this dichotomy is psychic in nature anyhow. The idea that objects have an independent and simultaneous existence gives rise to many of our concepts of time and space. For Jung, there was ultimately no real distinction here as evidenced by the following passage in The Structure and Dynamics of the Psyche:

> All that I experience is psychic. Even physical pain is a psychic image which I experience; my sense impressions--for all that they force upon me a world of impenetrable objects occupying space--are psychic images, and these alone are the immediate objects of my consciousness. My own psyche even transforms and falsifies reality, and it does this to such a degree that I must resort to artificial means to determine what things are like apart from myself. Then I discover that a sound is a vibration of air of such and such a frequency, or that a color is a wave of light of such and such a length. We are in truth so wrapped about by psychic images that we cannot penetrate at all to the essence of things external to ourselves. All our knowledge consists of the stuff of the psyche which, because it alone is immediate, is superlatively real.[24]

Jung, again, presses the point that:

> Far from being a material world, this is a psychic world, which allows us to make only indirect and hypothetical inferences about the real nature of matter. The psychic alone has immediate reality, and this includes all forms of the psychic, even "unreal" ideas and thought which refer to nothing "external." We may call them "imagination" or "delusion," but that does not

detract in any way from their effectiveness. Indeed, there is no "real" thought that cannot, at times, be thrust aside by an "unreal" one, thus proving that the latter is stronger and more effective than the former. Greater than all physical dangers are the tremendous effects of delusional ideas, which are yet denied all reality by our world-blinded consciousness. Our much vaunted reason and our boundlessly overestimated will are sometimes utterly powerless in the face of "unreal" thoughts. The world-powers that rule over all mankind, for good or ill, are unconscious psychic factors, and it is they that bring consciousness into being and hence create the sine qua non for the existence of any world at all. We are steeped in a world that was created by our own psyche.[25]

It is, then, quite unlikely that the scientific-technical arsenal of control, prediction, and measurement or rationalistic theory can completely provide the desiderata for investigating and understanding human nature. The polarized rationalistic conceptualization of human phenomena is inadequate because it is not based in experience, in the reality of the psyche. One often reads the findings of researchers which are absolutized or dogmatized while, at the same time, the formalism is presented as to the needs for additional research, for more information and study, in order to find the thing which was not really found in the first place. While this argument will be considered further in this essay, it is clear that a dogma, of whatever variety, is nothing in itself, although dogma can have a life of its own and a spirited, if not heated, disciplinary debate may be literally carried on over nothing.

All that is experienced is psychic at base. Reality for a human being is nonsense except as he or she participates in it, has some relationship to it, and is conscious of it. There is no actual distinction to be made between the psychic and the physical, or between organism and environment—the distinction is found in the thinking about the phenomenon, is found in the abstraction itself. The danger lies, not in the emergence of conscious from the unconscious, but in the complete separation of the two which has occurred in modern man; a separation reinforced by social scientific thinking. To see the world as separate from oneself, one must assume the illusory to be real. The unconscious must be assimilated to the ego. The examination of this problem is central to this essay. One must believe that one is characterized by a subject-object duality to sustain causality. Strictly speaking, however, the world is never separate from one except on the level of projection. "It" always implies an "I." Being implies non-being. Object implies subject; the two are inseparable, although social scientists carry out their researches as if they themselves were separate from the world, a "socially unattached intelligensia." Jung put the problem in an eloquent manner:

. . . unless we prefer to be made fools of by our illusions, we shall, by carefully analyzing every fascination, extract from a portion of our own personality, like a quintessence, and slowly come to recognize that we meet ourselves time and time again in a thousand disguises on the path of life.[26]

Of course, when a person is convinced that the source of emotion lies apparently in the other, in the environment, there is little desire to understand that this is a case of projection, to take true individual responsibility. This means that one has given oneself up to the projection. And, since unconsciousness rather than the conscious does the projecting, "one meets with one's projections, one does not make them."[27] Jung emphasizes that:

The effect of projection is to isolate the subject from his environment, since instead of a real relation to it there is now only an illusory one. Projections change the world into the replica of one's unknown face. In the last analysis, therefore, they lead to an autoerotic or autistic condition in which one dreams a world whose reality remains forever unattainable.[28]

Our concern with rationality is merely an aspect of the double-bind described initially. Social science has generally given itself up to the projection. In a sense, the more detailed our analyses become in a rational mode, the further we seem to be from life itself and the further we are from reason. The analysis presented by polarized rationality describes a dream world which cannot be. The highest and the lowest are denied. The self and shadow are consciously abolished. The shadow nevertheless demands its due and plagues one from without. The search for meaning which ensues and the consequent alienation which is experienced in the dream, becomes easily rationalized and located in a solely noxious environment rather than in oneself. Thus, the circle is established by which means the isolation and alienation become more acute.

The more projections are thrust in between the subject and the environment, the harder it is for the ego to see through its illusions . . . bewailing and cursing a faithless world that recedes further and further into the distance . . . it is an unconscious factor which spins the illusions that veil his world. And what is being spun as a cocoon, which in the end will completely envelop him.[29]

A rational, empirical social science is spinning such a cocoon. When rational explanation becomes one-sided, the ego is inflated and the unconscious is reduced to ego data and that which is beyond the ego is called illusion. Thus, reality is inverted, creating a second-order dream world which is, itself, an illusion of duality. One of the most pressing tasks of contemporary social science is to see through the boundaries unconsciously imposed in the pursuit of an unbalanced and rationalistic concept of human nature, to embark on the illumination of a new ethos.

An examination, brief at best, of Jung's psychology will lay the foundation for the analysis in Chapters IV and V concerning the crisis of political authority and the emergence of mass man, and the implications for the individual, for social science and for society. I, somewhat self-consciously, wish to preface the following chapter by noting that Jung did not particularly approve of summaries of his work, but since his ideas are not really very well understood among contemporary social scientists I feel that I must proceed nonetheless but with apologies to Jung and Jungians.

[1]T. S. Eliot, Four Quartets (New York: Harcourt, Brace & World, 1943), p. 58.

[2]Ernst Cassirer, Substance and Function and Einstein's Theory of Relativity (New York: Dover, 1953). Cassirer notes that physics, unlike the social sciences, has not been altogether unaware of this understanding.

> The new physical view proceeds neither from the assumption of a "space in itself"--it no longer recognizes space, force and matter as physical objects separated from each other, but . . . only the unity of certain functional relations, which are differently designated according to the system of reference in which we express them. (p. 398)

[3]C. G. Jung, Freud and Psychoanalysis, Bollingen Series XX, Collected Works, vol. 4 (Princeton: Princeton University Press, 1964), p. 400.

[4]Jung, The Structure and Dynamics of the Psyche, p. 436.

[5]Ernst Cassirer, The Logic of the Humanities (New Haven: Yale University Press, 1961), pp. 36-37:

> We are incapable of anticipating the future development of civilization. Nor can it be completely understood through any amount of empirical knowledge of its past and present. . . . Human action is known only in its own realization.

[6]Jung, The Structure and Dynamics of the Psyche, p. 414.

[7]Ibid., pp. 414-415.

[8]Jung, "Synchronicity: An Acausal Connecting Principle," in The Structure and Dynamics of the Psyche, pp. 422-423.

[9]Jung, The Structure and Dynamics of the Psyche, p. 247.

[10]Ibid., p. 435.

[11]Ibid., pp. 435-436.

[12]Ibid., p. 441.

[13]Ibid., p. 436.

[14]Ibid., p. 444.

[15]Ibid., p. 445.

[16]Ibid., pp. 445-446.

[17]Jung, The Undiscovered Self, p. 19.

[18]Ibid., p. 18.

[19]Jung, The Structure and Dynamics of the Psyche, p. 731.

[20]Jung, Psychological Types, p. 60.

[21]Wittgenstein concurred with Jung:

> For an answer which cannot be expressed the question
> too cannot be expressed. The riddle does not exist. If
> a question can be put at all, then it can also be said.
> We feel that even if all possible scientific questions be
> answered, the problems of life have still not been
> touched at all. Of course there is then no question left,
> and just this is the answer. The solution of the problem
> of life is seen in the vanishing of this problem. (Is not
> this the reason why men to whom after long doubting
> the sense of life became clear, could not then say
> wherein this sense consisted?)

Ludwig Wittgenstein, Tractatus Logico-Philosophicus (London: Routledge
and Kegan Paul, 1960), ref. 10, 6.5, 6.51, 6.52, 6.521, emphasis mine. It
should be noted that there are two Wittgensteins. One is a defender of
science, and the other is the philosopher who sees the same problems Jung
has articulated.

[22]Jung, Analytical Psychology: Its Theory and Practice, p. 7. Also,
in reference to the relation between the states of the nervous system and
ego-consciousness, see: Jung, The Structure and Dynamics of the Psyche,
pp. 324ff.

[23]Jung, The Structure and Dynamics of the Psyche, p. 529.

[24]Ibid., p. 353.

[25]Ibid., p. 747.

[26]C. G. Jung, "The Psychology of the Transference," in The Practice
of Psychotherapy, Bollingen Series XX, Collected Works, vol. 16 (Princeton: Princeton University Press, 1966), p. 156.

[27]Jung, _Aion_, p. 9.   For an excellent summary of the Shadow archetype, see Chapter II in _Aion_.

[28]Jung, _Aion_, p. 9.

[29]Ibid., pp. 9-10.

CHAPTER III

JUNG'S SYMBOLIC PSYCHOLOGY

> Paradox . . . does more justice to the <u>unknowable</u> than
> clarity can do, for uniformity of <u>meaning</u> robs the
> mystery of its darkness and sets it up as something that
> is <u>known</u>. That is a usurpation, and it leads the human
> <u>intellect</u> into hubris by pretending that it, the intellect,
> has got hold of the transcendent mystery by a cognitive
> act and "grasped" it. The paradox therefore reflects a
> higher level of intellect and, by not forcibly represent-
> ing the unknowable as known, gives a more faithful
> picture of the real state of affairs.[1]

While Jung speaks of patterns and structures of the psyche, it is
clear that these were not intended as static categories, but should be
taken in a symbolic sense thus embracing the reality of the paradox which
Jung thought was a more accurate representation of human nature. The
psyche is a continually unfolding potentiality. The most essential
assumption with regard to the human psyche that Jung makes is that of
a pattern which is susceptible only to symbolic interpretation because it
is greater than consciousness or the specific ego conscious mode of
intellection. Given the rationalist tendency within the social sciences,
the attempt to grasp the meaning of symbolism is difficult because it
does not seem "real." Rationalism does not orient itself toward matters
which exceed the bounds of consensual fact and logic. In fact, intuition,
feeling, and emotion, as well as unconsciousness have been largely
disregarded or smothered with rationalizations which actually accentuate
incertitude if the rationalism is rigidly held. Logic or fact alone cannot
touch or motivate these experiences. Neither can sense data. Jung's
understanding of the symbol is an expression of his primary notion of the
essential wholeness of the psyche. And the symbol is the best possible
representation of something as yet unknown and unfathomable. The
symbol of the wholeness-entirety is the focus or heart of the organizing
principle of the psyche, and this image of completeness is the compensation to uncertainty, anxiety, alienation, and confusion. It is in this sense
that Jung touches the process which allows the discovery of the Self
beyond the social scientific self. An exploration in which all scholars
might engage themselves.

Self exploration is the essence of the analytical process in Jung's
psychology. This path is called the way of individuation and is the process
of the realization of Self, a searching for Self knowledge. In this process
one becomes whole, integrating all of the conscious and inchoate
possibilities in the person. The nature of the individuation process is such

that it involves one in the rejection of collective conventions as well as preconceived orthodox attitudes which characterize mundane reality for most people. As such, the individuation process bears political implications. In this sense, Jung's psychology is iconoclastic, but the process does not end in nihilism with the destruction of all that is conventional. The art of seeing through ego-conscious constructions leads instead to a higher level of understanding—the plane of the Self. Perhaps the most beautiful expression of the process of searching is to be found in the verses of T. S. Eliot:

> We shall not cease from exploration
> And the end of all our exploring
> Will be to arrive where we started
> And know the place for the first time.
> Through the unknown, remembered gate
> When the last of earth left to discover
> Is that which was the beginning;
> At the source of the longest river
> The voice of the hidden waterfall
> And the children in the apple-tree
> Not known, because not looked for
> But heard, half-heard, in the stillness
> Between two waves of the sea.[2]

The process of individuation, becoming one's Self, carries the possibility of a higher understanding. It is an exploration of the ageless imperative of "Know thyself!" It is also a most difficult question. Who am I?

Jung may have provided the basis for a reconceptualization of human nature which would allow the contemporary social sciences to rescue perspective. If one cannot enter into the exploration, then one has scant hope of knowing one's Self, let alone human nature. For how could one know others without knowing oneself? Individuation is a way of liberation, of emancipation from the illusions of a second order reality. Is this not the scholar's goal traditionally? In principle, if not in fact? If solutions for social issues or political issues are to be proposed, do such proposals not flow from the values of the individual? How would it be possible to make a wise judgment about values if that judgment were clouded with illusion? Or if one were unaware of the unconscious? Yet the social sciences appear to be remarkably naive here. The individuation process is a process whereby in becoming wise about one's Self, one may become wise about the world and other people. One would imagine that we all have our hands full in becoming ourselves by understanding our Self; that pronouncements about the nature of other human beings in ignorance of ourselves can only be an act of hubris. Before one can change the world, one must be able to change oneself. The theory or method, which captures the attention of so many, does not matter here, it is secondary, for the crucial factor is the wisdom of the individual. "In reality," said Jung,

. . . everything depends on the man and little or nothing on the method. For the method is merely the path, the direction taken by a man. The way he acts is the true expression of his nature. If it ceases to be this, then the method is nothing more than an affectation, something artificially added, rootless, and sapless, serving only the illegitimate goal of deception.[3]

Much of the implicit commentary by social scientists as to the nature of human beings is unconsciously deceptive, perpetuating illusion rather than nurturing and building up life; attempting to close the exit from identification with collective ideals and collective norms. This is largely unconscious—the social scientist does not think of himself in this light. The humane role of the social scientist could be to help people to see through the deception, but this would, of course, be impossible if the social scientist himself were deceived and required the approval of outside agencies for his life orientation. One's being is enormously subjective and the understanding of the paradox of human nature, of "a more faithful picture," must start with oneself, not with the "average," "ideal" or "other person." Perhaps social science has much to learn from Jung here.

Symbols do not come from the outside, but are latent in unconsciousness. External events may activate a symbol, but symbols are not consciously created as are signs which stand for something known. It is possible, of course, to degrade symbols, but once a symbol has been emptied of meaning, it cannot be resurrected from the outside. Symbols are instead the spontaneous representations of the unconscious. For a symbol to last, it must be connected to meaningful experience within the preconscious spheres of the individual psyche. The particular form that a symbol may assume is the link between that which is transcendent and that which is historical. Unconsciousness is, again, in its simplest understanding, <u>unknown.</u> An authentic symbol is not something which can be subject to social consensus or fabrication since <u>a symbol represents a</u> <u>spontaneous experience which points beyond the symbol to an under-</u> <u>standing or meaning which cannot be put into merely rational terms.</u> Jung states:

> [A symbol] is not an arbitrary or intentional sign standing for a known and conceivable fact, but an admittedly anthropormorphic—hence limited and only partly valid—expression for something suprahuman and only partly conceivable. It may be the best expression possible, yet it ranks below the level of the mystery it seeks to describe.[4]

> An expression that stands for a known thing always remains merely a sign, and is never a symbol. It is, therefore, quite impossible to make a living symbol, i.e., one that is pregnant with meaning, from known associations.[5]

41

The distinction between symbol and sign is an important one. Conceptualizations, as such, are products of intentional and conscious mental activity and are never expressive of the unconscious or the Self except as partial actualizations. Rational and conscious models of human nature are likewise not expressive of meaning in symbolic terms. Nor, one might add, are they likely to become truly symbolic of the human psyche since their integrity depends upon external objects; depends upon a politics of knowledge. A representation of the human being is only a skeleton of human wholeness when it is derived only through sensation and intellection. It is quite important to understand this symbolic approach since it is essential to Jung's psychology. To reduce the symbol to a rationalism, a logical sign, would be a misunderstanding of Jung and, in fact, defeat the meanings available. Symbols which emerge naturally from unconsciousness are attempts to describe the situation of a human being or culture in terms of parallels or analogues rather than what is known as factual or rational or objective terms. A symbol goes beyond itself and points to the unknown. It is, in a certain sense, a metaphor. Of course, symbols in their psychological form emerge spontaneously from unconsciousness into conscious attitudes. From the social perspective, symbols turn the energy of an individual to the activities of the group, and from the historical perspective, the symbol will appear in variety—its form will change from culture to culture through time.[6]

Symbols are indicative of the unknown elements or aspects of the psyche that are unconscious. Both "conscious" and "unconscious" have to do with the individual and one's subjective states, but to be conscious is to be aware, to discriminate, to have thoughts or feelings about something. Unconscious makes reference to inner experiencing of which the individual is not aware in a discriminate manner. Things, in a sense, become unconscious when they are ignored or repressed. Things remain unconscious when the individual loses the sense of meaning and fullness associated with the symbols of the psyche. The adoption of rationalist methodologies with the corresponding emphasis upon a sensory and intellectual Weltanschauung speaks only to the limited and not to the symbol. The solution, although the experience of reason clearly goes from compactness to differentiation, is not merely to extend the senses, as in the case of more and more elaborate scientific and rationalistic instrumentation, nor is it to extend the intellect in its rationalistic sense as in the case of more and more elaborate computer technology—the network still remains, and "reality" is found in the structures of the network itself. The unconscious cannot be derived from test scores regardless of their type any more than can quality be quantified since once this has happened it is no longer a quality. Yet this is the character of our time and culture with its quantitative and material bias.

It is very difficult to see that objective experience is merely a second-order expression of the reality it describes, and that the fact of authentic intersubjectivity remains. One of the unconscious problems of the rationalist perspective is that consciousness is out of touch with value and the intuitive and unconscious roots of life and reason which is an impoverishment. This is an account of human nature without meaning.

42

Of course this may be an advantage of sorts as the King in <u>Alice in Wonderland</u> noted: "If there's no meaning in it, . . . that saves a world of trouble, you know, as we needn't try to find any." Jung's view of the unconscious was that it ultimately contained profound wisdom; a wisdom that was beyond the capacity of ego consciousness to understand. Jung did not feel compelled to reject a notion simply because it was not susceptible to rational proof—the existence of the psyche and its contents does not require proof since it is real and immediate; none of us, one trusts, doubts our existence. Inasmuch as we are conscious of our individual existence, we thereby transcend it. Jung is careful to point out that the "unconscious is not simply the unknown, it is rather the unknown psychic."[7] Unconsciousness, to Jung, is a different instrumentality than the conscious. The form of consciousness itself is systematized in manners that may be regarded as potentially infinite, and those manifestations will be in terms of the states of the nervous system or the systematizations or ideologies which organize cognition.[8] The socio-political implication of unconsciousness is based primarily in the socialization of individuals into the form of that particular social system which is an organizing of consciousness with penalties for the individual. Jung writes about the security symbol:

> The performance of a "magical" action gives the person concerned a feeling of security which is absolutely essential for carrying out a decision, because a decision is inevitably somewhat one-sided and is therefore rightly felt to be a risk. Even a dictator thinks it necessary not only to accompany his acts of State with threats but to stage them with all manner of solemnities. Brass bands, flags, banners, parades and monster demonstrations are not different in principle from ecclesiastical processions, cannonades and fireworks to scare off demons. Only, the suggestive parade of State power engenders a collective feeling of security which, unlike religious demonstrations, gives the individual no protection against his inner demonism. Hence he will cling all the more to the power of the State, i.e., to the mass, thus delivering himself up to it psychically as well as morally and putting the finishing touch to his social depotentiation.[9]

Keeping in mind that "the system" is a form of categorical magic, survival is achieved, according to the popular conception, for the social system by ignoring personal or individual experience and thus luring the individual into identification with systemic notions of the good social order or with notions of the ideal personality. The social or political system acts as a socio-political filter, spinning a fantasy that is a second-order expression and thus illusory.[10]

There are at least two major consequences of the acceptance of the second-order expression in the sense being discussed: first, one is taught fictions about reality which become included in ego-consciousness; and second, actual reality is kept from coming into consciousness as one's attention is externally focused upon the objects of consciousness. I do not mean to imply that such fictions should, or could, be abandoned, but rather that political systems always govern most effectively at the level of the unconscious. Thus political scientists could gain great understanding of politics by exploring the unconscious, thus exploring subliminal politics.

All social or political "systems" have, of course, classes or categories pertaining to what passes for "sane" experience or "ideal personality" which inform one as to "reality" and as to deviance from the rule of the herd. These forms are inextricably related to the form of thoughts, and of sensations such as seeing, feeling, hearing, and so forth. Linguistically, one might say that experience is socially or politically conditioned by the form of a given language, by its syntax, grammatical construction and the definitions of the words. That is, in a sense, the world is made up of words which are, in turn, related to the form of consciousness. The reasoning processes of a given culture are also socially conditioned modes. The rational conscious mode is dominant and tends to reduce the unconscious to the rational. Again, it may be suggested that there exists a politics of knowledge. Paradoxical thinking, on the other hand, would understand consciousness and nonconsciousness not to exclude one another as predicates of human nature.

The social or political system places an emphasis on described experiences which are considered to be of value or acceptable in terms of the systematization itself. Most of our notions of deviance flow from this fact, and therefore some experiences must be repressed when particular forms of awareness are incompatible with the social consensus or predominant notions of the ideal social order and ideal personality. To place great importance on conventions one has, in effect, contrived a comfortable manner of obtaining one's decisions so that reliance on one's self is avoided. Unconscious human beings are fundamentally herd animals. What conventions do is to maintain people in an unconscious state so that they are relieved of the necessity of individually rendering conscious and responsible decisions. Progroff says that the release from the making of decisions, ". . . this very convenience, this ease with which routine can be substituted for deliberated action, is the greatest psychological danger of all."[11] The danger resides in the unpredictable consequences which may arise when novel circumstances which do not fit the social, or intellectual, conventions occur. The context is one in which people may feel fear and anxiety, in which attempted survival becomes of ultimate importance and the possibility for the entrance of a charismatic leader to rekindle the spirit of the people is enhanced. The routines of a bureaucratized social system, of course, provide an aggravated example of the ease with which individual responsibility for taking decisions can be avoided. The example of Nazi Germany, "where the vast majority turned to the regimentation and mass murders of a demonic, charismatic leader, perhaps to satisfy a gnawing hunger for meaning in a bureaucratized society," cannot, in good faith, be taken lightly by social scientists.[12]

44

This episode cannot be characterized as merely German or as anomalous. The danger for the individual is the loss of his soul. The examples of mass murder and destructive collective movements abound and are to be found at all times in all cultures.

Many of the elements of the personal unconscious are a result of repression or aversion to pain. Responses to a conscious circumstance, State policies for example, where the response is not noticed or is unconscious, constitute repression. Many of those things which are repressed are painful feelings or thoughts. Thus, repression, while closely related to forgetting and ignoring, is the manner in which problems can be circumvented that would otherwise appear to threaten the stability of ego-consciousness. It is important to note, experiencially, that repression is something that happens to a person, not something which one does. Thus, the unconscious is outside as well. In the same manner, as a result of repression or the maintenance of unconscious elements, one projects characteristics onto other persons or circumstances which, in reality, find their source in terms of intra-psychic phenomena. Thus, people encounter their projections, they do not, strictly speaking, make projections. Again, this carries political and social import. To ignore the inner source of the odd things which occur is somewhat hazardous, since:

> Once the symptoms are really outside in some form of sociopolitical insanity, it is impossible to convince anybody that the conflict is in the psyche of every individual, since he is quite sure where his enemy is. Then, the conflict, which remains an intra-psychic phenomenon in the mind of the discerning person, takes place on the plane of projection in the form of political tension and murderous violence. To produce such consequences, the inidivdual must have been thoroughly indoctrinated with the insignificance and worthlessness of his psyche.[13]

Projection occurs through the unconscious, not the conscious subject, which has the effect of isolating a person from his environment due to the deceptive appearance which characterizes the relationship. "Projections," Jung states, "change the world into a replica of one's unknown face."[14] Projections involve isolation, alienation, anxiety and fear, and

> lead to an autoerotic or autistic condition in which one dreams a world whose reality remains forever unattainable. The resultant sentiment d'incompletude and the still worse feeling of sterility are in their turn explained by projection as the malevolence of the environment, and by means of this vicious circle the isolation is intensified. The more projections interpose themselves between the subject and the environment, the harder it becomes for the ego to see through its illusions.[15]

The Self

Jung is emphatic that the concept of the Self is only "the hypothetical summation of an indescribable totality."[16] The Self, as used by Jung, is not to be confused with the concept of the rationalized self found in most academic psychological and sociological literature. The self in the case of the social sciences would be more closely analogous to what Jung refers to as the ego, a constituent of consciousness. While this may not seem to be a very important point, it is, in fact, quite central to understanding Jung's exegesis of the psyche, for the limitations of the self to the realm of ego-consciousness is merely intellectual, and Jung presses the point that

> The intellectual "grasp" of a psychological fact produces no more than a concept of it, and . . . a concept is no more than a name, a flatus vocis. These intellectual counters can be bandied about easily enough . . . for they have no weight or substance. . . . The intellect is undeniably useful in its own field, but is a great cheat and illusionist outside of it whenever it tries to manipulate values.[17]

In other words, the concept is useless if it does not bear authentic relationship to the engendering experience--if it is not understood as an expression of the non-dual Self. The concept itself is only the means to account for something or to indicate a given summation of experience. Only additional experience can illuminate the reality. To bog oneself down in this second-order expression of concepts is misleading since

> Philosophical criticism will find everything to object to in them unless it begins by recognizing that they are concerned with facts, and that the "concept" is simply an abbreviated description or definition of these facts. Such criticism has as little effect on the object as zoological criticism on a duck-billed platypus. It is not the concept that matters; the concept is only a word, a counter, and it has meaning and use only because it stands for a certain sum of experience.[18]

The Self is symbolic of the absolute, and in this sense is the ultimate archetype (symbol) referring to the non-dual. This is not the same as "personality," not the self as in myself, herself, himself, and so forth, since these latter concepts are all references to ego-consciousness. As a symbolic representation of the awareness underlying thought and feeling, the Self is awareness itself, and, as such, is the background from which individual experience and ego-consciousness emerge as secondary expressions--as the objects of awareness.

Clearly then, the Self, as Jung meant it, does not correspond with the contemporary usage in the social sciences. Since the Self is not the same as the ego because it encompasses the ego, so to speak, it is manifested in consciousness and unconsciousness through meaningful correspondences rather than through the laws of cause and effect. What does this mean for the social scientist? It means that the language of the psyche cannot be the same as that of the natural sciences which is causal or probablistic. Causal language would not permit an understanding of the Self. The Self is experienced as wholeness and is therefore not identical with the ego as the center of consciousness. Jung defends his own use of the Self as a notion that is essentially symbolic:

> Consciousness is phylogenetically and ontogenetically a secondary phenomenon. It is time this obvious fact were grasped at last. Just as the body has an anatomical prehistory of millions of years, so also does the psychic system . . . the psyche of the child in its preconscious state is anything but a tabula rasa; it is already preformed in a recognizably individual way, and is moreover equipped with all specifically human instincts, as well as with the a priori foundations of the higher functions. On this complicated base, the ego arises. Throughout life the ego is sustained by this base. When the base does not function, stasis ensues and then death. Its life and its reality are of vital importance. Compared to it, even the external world is secondary, for what does the world matter if the endogenous impulse to grasp it and manipulate it is lacking? In the long run no conscious will can ever replace the life instinct. This instinct comes to us from within, as a compulsion or will or command, and if--as has more or less been done from time immemorial--we give it the name of a personal daimon we are at least aptly expressing the psychological situation. And if, by employing the concept of the archetype, we attempt to define a little more closely the point at which the daimon grips us, we have not abolished anything, only approached closer to the source of life.[19]

The Self is not the center of consciousness, but is the archetype of human wholeness and is, in a certain sense, neither within nor without, but is beyond and thus transcendent of ego-consciousness. The path to the Self, to repeat, is what Jung called the individuation process. The ego, on the other hand, tends to preserve the consistency and prevailing circumstances of consciousness, of the personality and its accompanying value hierarchies and is a "secondary phenomenon." This tendency has very important results in terms of politics; and these consequences will be elaborated in chapters four and five.

The attempt to acquire solutions to the problems of life or politics through ego-consciousness is not possible--that is, we should not have the idea that these problems are solvable. We cannot consciously fit nonconscious elements into consciousness. One, in other words, cannot "try" to relate the two sides. The Self, to Jung's mind, however, guides the

47

process of individuation when the conscious claim to complete control is given up.[20] However, the social sciences have tended to conceive of human nature as merely ego-consciousness or ego-psychology. This prevalent view transforms the human being into a thing which is not as problematic and filled with paradoxes as is the reality. The conceptualization of the Self in terms of ego-consciousness within the scope of a rationalist social science is the process of narrowing down the human being until only an insignificant average quantity or moral type remains. When this occurs, the actual individual is seen as lifeless--as a social unit. In this sense, our theories are permeated with death. Jung wrote that "concepts are coined and negotiable values; images are life."[21] Inasmuch as social science remains only rationalistic, life may be known, but it is not understood. It is not understood because in our pursuit of social and political goals the psychology of the human being who is to be the recipient of the goals is ignored because, most likely, the policy-maker does not understand himself in the first place. It would seem that through the process of reification, a social-psychological reality of the second-order expression can be created which in fact denies authentic human existence. The denial of life, however, is also the denial of death. This fallacy of concreteness carries no compassion. the notion that ego-consciousness is the totality of the human psyche is merely an eidolon of the conscious mind.

Ego Inflation and Political Behavior

The Self can be likened to an a priori existent. As a representation, the Self allows us to examine and reflect on experiences which include a dynamic relation between ego-consciousness and other contents of the psyche. The reduction of the transpersonal to the ego results in ego inflation. This is an important consideration and Jung points out that the failure to grant the existence of psychic contents beyond ego-consciousness is not without consequence.

> The more numerous and the more significant the unconscious contents which are assimilated to the ego, the closer the approximation of the ego to the self, even though this approximation must be a never-ending process. This inevitably produces an inflation of the ego. . . . To psychologize this reality out of existence either is ineffectual, or else merely increases the inflation of the ego. One cannot dispose of facts by declaring them unreal.[22]

Ego inflation means that one is merged with the projection-making factor. "Inflation magnifies the blind spot in the eye."[23] The more one is merged with the projection-making factor, the more likely one is to identify with it. This is the danger of assimilation (the reduction of the non-dual self to duality in terms of ego-consciousness) in the sense that the denial of the fact of projection means identification with it. Inasmuch as one rationalizes the Self or the contents of unconsciousness in terms of ego-consciousness, the Self is assimilated to the ego and ego inflation occurs. The more rigidly a scholar held to a solely rational explanation, the more blind the scholar would become. Jung has in his work commented extensively on the dynamic relation between consciousness and unconsciousness in terms of psychic inflation and the influences on political behaviors as conscious assimilation of unconscious content occurs. Jung argues that mass movements and mass psychoses are the result of this inflation of the ego. When this is the case, writes Jung,

> The goal and meaning of individual life (which is the only real life) no longer lie in individual development but in the policy of the State, which is thrust upon the individual from outside and consists in the execution of an abstract idea which ultimately tends to attract all life to itself.[24]

> . . . in order to compensate for its chaotic formlessness, a mass always produces a "Leader," who almost infallibly becomes the victim of his own inflated ego-consciousness, as numerous examples in history show.[25]

It would seem that people have a tendency to either imitate the creations of ego-consciousness or allow themselves to be conditioned to identify with the products of ego-consciousness. Scientific rationalism bolsters these tendencies as the individual, through the socialization process, comes to believe that the rational second-order expressions of human nature are in fact real. The Self symbol has been inverted at this point—reduced to a mere sign. As the sources of the identity become more and more external, and thus further and further removed from what one actually is, the meaning of life is lost. The path of emancipation is hidden. This, needless to say, coincides with an immortality problem as one is sundered from the dimension of life itself. This is the alienation of a highly rationalized society. It could also be the precursor of very destructive social and political movements. It simply means that as the sociopolitical concepts of the ego-conscious self are substituted for the symbolic Self, many people may become adjuncts of the State or the social order. Thus, rationalism is not only instrumental, it also bears political content.

> In this way the individual becomes more and more a function of society, which in its turn usurps the function of the real life carrier, whereas, in actual fact, society is nothing more than an abstract idea like the State. Both are hypostatized, that is, have become autonomous. The State in particular is turned into a quasi-animate personality from whom everything is expected. In reality it is only a camouflage for those individuals who know how to manipulate it.[26]

The State is, of course, an abstract postulate of order, although the abstract postulate of order has many faces. Under conditions of psychic inflation, individual differences or deviances tend not to be tolerated—social, psychological, and political uniformity is demanded. These demands may be seen even within the democratic states. It is demanded in terms of the ideal personality or, in periods of instability, in terms of the good social order. This will inevitably produce counter-ideologies. The consequence, in any case, is the atrophy of the individual psyche and its limitation to externally designated roles and status.[27] The individuation process, the exploration for the truth or Self, is greatly hindered, although the life instinct will always urge the individual to go beyond the ego consciousness, so one is never beyond hope or redemption.

There are, obviously, cases of identification with social roles which correspond with the atrophy of the individual psyche among members of the subcultural groups, racial groups, or segments of the lower classes. That is, we may also speak of deflation. Identification with such roles, as they are defined by the second-order realities, imposes an impoverished view of the psyche which affects not only consciousness, but unconsciousness as well. The socialization process often creates the second-order reality in which a person can become thusly confused. The following is obviously an example of what might be termed, in distinction to psychic inflation, psychic deflation:

> A middle-class Negro woman, herself light, on giving
> birth to a dark baby . . . was sure she had been given
> the wrong baby; later she tried to bathe it in bleaches
> of various kinds; she refused to appear in public with it.
> She reacted almost the same way with a second baby.[28]

"Consciousness," writes Jung, "is very much the product of perception and orientation in the external world."[29] The collective conscious that derives from the assimilation of unconsciousness to the ego is made of all our statistical truths, average truths, conventionality, opinionation, rationalism, and banal moralities. The attraction to these conventionalities comes from the fear and consequent repression of the unconscious, the uncertain, and the unknown. "There are far more people," remarked Jung, "who are afraid of the unconscious than one would suspect. They are even afraid of their own shadow."[30] In this sense, the mass is not as evolved as the individuals who comprise the mass, rather it "is the sum total of individuals in need of redemption."[31] Projection of unconscious elements cements the individual to the group since the group will, at this point, contain an integral segment of the psychology of the individual. Remembering that what is unconscious will be projected, Jung illuminates the problem by simply writing that: ". . . in so far as society itself is composed of de-individualized persons, it is completely at the mercy of ruthless individuals."[32]

Ego-consciousness is further analyzed by Jung. The persona, or mask that one presents to the world, can be analytically distinguished from the ego. The persona is the "deal" or compromise an individual makes between the requirements of society and the willfulness of the ego and its corresponding personality structure. It is the ideal personality presented in social interaction. As the ego becomes identified with the persona, some spontaneous aspects of the personality fall into unconsciousness, creating a shadow personality. The consequence is the taking on of the persona as a part of the collective unconscious. Jung's representation for this aspect of unconsciousness is the Shadow archetype, our dark, closeted side. Still the life instinct moves toward the Self. The Self is a tendency toward the union of consciousness and unconsciousness—the whole of psychic entirety. The Self is the center of awareness which the ego moves round about as a subordinate factor. This subordinate factor is the self (personality) of the social sciences. The social sciences would do well to understand this.

The Ego Complex

"The ego," writes Jung, "rests on the total field of consciousness," as well as "on the sum total of unconscious contents."[33] The ego, however, is not made up of the "field of consciousness," but it is the focus or point of reference of consciousness. This, needless to say, presents a problem—a critical one—namely, that the psyche is both the subject and the object of study. Jung denotes the ego as follows:

> We understand the ego as the complex factor to which all conscious contents are related. It forms, as it were, the centre of the field of consciousness; and, in so far as this comprises the empirical personality, the ego is the subject of all personal acts of consciousness. The relation of a psychic content to the ego forms the criterion of its consciousness, for no content can be conscious unless it is presented to a subject.[34]

The ego, then, can be considered the subject within the phenomenal world of "things." Jung reasons that two classes of unknown objects can occur to ego-consciousness: one, external objects which are not known through the senses; and, second, unknowns which are immediately experienced internally, and are understood as unconscious. These unknowns are the limits to consciousness. The categorization of unknowns into these two classes is useful, but not a solution to the problem since whatever one assumes to be will be found outside oneself. Perhaps this is an obscure manner in which to say that the ego is actually a complex which, in a "circumambulatory" way, one can speak of as the center of individual identity and consciousness. But a center with limits, so to speak. The fact remains, nonetheless, that Jung himself confessed that "the nature of consciousness is a riddle whose solution I do not know."[35] Jung writes that the ego "would never amount to more than a picture of the conscious personality; all those features which are unknown or unconscious to the subject would be missing."[36] The ego is not the total—the total is understood by the symbol of the Self as discussed previously and the ego is subordinate to the Self. The very uniqueness of the individual makes the ego difficult to speak about even though we claim to have accumulated knowledge concerning the ego. Jung does not help to solve this problem, although he encourages understanding, as he acknowledges that:

> The ego, ostensibly the thing we know most about, is in fact a highly complex affair full of unfathomable obscurities. Indeed, one could even define it as a relatively constant personification of the unconscious itself, or as the Schopenhaurian mirror in which the unconscious becomes aware of its own face.[37]

It may be helpful to understand the ego in terms of the sum of physical and mental features which are characteristic of individual existence and the consciousness of this separate, corporeal existence. In fact, it may be very helpful to understand the ego as a partial manifestation of the life mystery. The Self transcends the ego, therefore one may reflect on the ego. Inasmuch as one is conscious of something, there is a distinction to be made between consciousness and the object of consciousness. Once again, as one is conscious of individual existence, one transcends it. It is this transcendence, this Self-reflection, which is dismissed by a rationalistic social science as only metaphysics, perhaps philosophy or theory, but not science.

The ego may be viewed as the subject and object of personal identity--an identity which would be involved in, but not entirely explicable in terms of, the dimensions of time, space, and causality. In this same sense, the ego seems to be the focus of personal decisions. In other words, the state of ego-consciousness is the state of duality--in fact, Jung often uses the term ego-consciousness because consciousness in the Jungian sense and the ego are dependent upon on another. The ego, then, is a complex of identity susceptible to fragmentation and change. The ego is mutable. The Self is not. The ego is a partial manifestation in personality of the Self, which is itself beyond space and time. The ego is a partially actualized and limited expression of psychic totality. This, of course, means that the notion that the ego is the dominant entity is an egotism itself and therefore illusory.[38] Ego cannot see ego. The Self is in contradistinction, so to speak, to the ego as a seemingly a priori totality symbol. The ego, in terms of personality, is the conditioned "I." As the ego is conditioned, it is again subject to fragmentation and changeability for its character is merged with externalities of a world which itself ever changes.

The ego is a limited actualization of the Self and occurs in consciousness as identification with the somatic or mental occurs.[39] In so far as ego-consciousness rests upon the senses, conditioning can occur. There are several somatic bases for such conditioning of the ego. The experience of the body as it is separated from the mother at birth may, for example, produce an elementary image of individual separateness and existential anxiety as nonduality becomes an experience divided into subject and object. This initial separation may provide a basis for the

52

development of ego-consciousness.[40] In the same line of thinking, the problem of inferiority and the complementary will to power might seem to be a rather natural consequence of the confrontation of an omnipotent, omnipresent, and omniscient (and, perhaps, omnivorous) adult world.[41] Freud's notions of infantile sexuality and body self-image are also components of ego development. But, when the ego is confronted with change or uncertainty, as must naturally occur, anxiety results. The ego then seeks to maintain itself as the dominant factor. To remain dominant, that which is beyond the ego, the Self, must be denied by the ego. The reality of psychic realms beyond ego control are denied. The denial of the existential ground of life itself is motivated by Phobos, the ego's fear of death, which is coincidental in meaning with the fear of life. Unconsciously, fear of death is the repression of the life instinct.

The ego is duality. The Self is nondual or the "not-I."[42] The ego, however, should not be regarded as being outside the Self--the only separation that can actually be made is analytical. The growth of the ego structure is "the process of becoming aware of one's own being as a separate unit of humanity."[43] As human beings, we exist, so to speak, in the seeming tension of the dual and the nondual. June Singer elaborates:

> From the point of view of the ego, growth and development depend on integrating into the sphere of the ego as much as possible of that which was formerly unknown. This unconscious content comprises two categories. The first is knowledge of the world and the way it works; basically this is a function of education of both the formal kind (schooling) and the informal kind (empirical experience). The second category is wisdom; this is essentially the understanding of human nature including one's own nature as an individual. Thus the goal of the individuation process as seen from the standpoint of the ego, is the expansion of awareness.

> From the point of view of the Self, however, the goal of individuation is quite different. Where the ego was oriented toward its own emergence from the unconscious, the self is oriented toward union of consciousness with unconscious. It may be said that life begins with the ego in the ascendency, as the infant begins to wrest knowledge from the vast realms of the unknown. . . . But ultimately each life ends with the defeat of the ego.[44]

And so must each life come to terms with death. The ways of masking the death question are, however, multitudinous.

Jung denotes what he calls the Persona which is contained within the complex of ego-consciousness. The term "persona" was, of course, the Latin word for mask. It was an appropriate choice as the persona masks the inner life of a person in terms of social interaction. The social system requires categories of convenience into which a person may be put or will put himself. Since a person will usually attempt to be represented in society in the most favorable terms possible, the persona is the ideal of one's personality--the conscious ideal. Persona will, quite naturally, take different forms with different individuals. The most notable characteristic of the persona is that it is of ego-consciousness--that is, persona is a conscious attitude. As such, it is in relationship to unconsciousness and the elements of the persona are balanced by elements in unconsciousness--any excessive attitude manifested by the persona will be matched by the excessive opposite attitude in unconsciousness--the Shadow. "Whoever builds up too good a persona," comments Jung, "has to pay for it in irritability."[45] In a sense, the ego builds what is felt to be the favorable aspects of the personality while the less favorable aspects fall into unconsciousness. This "other side" is referred to by Jung as the Shadow and it has an autonomous existence. The Shadow is composed of those things that are not approved of in terms of the conscious attitude, but which enter into consciousness periodically--Jung describes this circumstance by saying, "an opposite is forced up from within; it is exactly as though the unconscious suppressed the ego with a force equal to that which drew the ego into the persona."[46] The tendency for the Shadow, not only to interfere in one's conscious life, but also to be projected onto others is great. It is in this sense that we are able to see our own worst weaknesses and faults in other people. Freud's pre-occupation with the evil tendencies to be found in the unconscious was a concentration on the Shadow. Jung understood this and remarked:

> The end-product of the Freudian method is a detailed elaboration of man's shadow. . . . The horror which we feel for Freudian interpretations is entirely due to our own barbaric or childish naivete, which believes that there can be heights without corresponding depths and which blinds us to the really "final" truth that carried to extremes, opposites meet. Our mistake would lie in supposing that what is radiant no longer exists because it has been explained from the shadow-side.[47]

The conflict between the Persona and the Shadow has a sociopolitical analogue. The ego resists assimilating shadow qualities and thus they exist on the level of projection and the evil and the threatening are located in others. At the level of the nation, the Shadow is located analogously with other nations, with the enemy. Jung observed:

> The psychology of war has clearly brought this condition to light: everything which our nation does is good, everything which the other nations do is wicked. The centre of all that is mean and vile is always to be found several miles behind the enemy's lines.[48]

The withdrawal of the projections is difficult because the ego resists the inevitable change in the nature of ego identification which must surely follow from such a course.

54

Anxiety with regard to change and its political implications is the substance of the following sections. As earlier elaborated, ego-consciousness appears to be somatically grounded, yet consists of thoughts and feelings as well. Anxiety can occur therefore not only when the body itself is threatened, but also when the sense of personal identity is threatened. Any deep psychological change in which ego-consciousness itself is involved has, as its experiential counterpart, the experience of death to some degree. The fact that life, rebirth, may follow bearing the possibility of a greatly enriched life of the individual is not seen from the point of view of the ego which seeks to remain the center of control. The fear involved in the threat to the body/mind is the fear of dissolution, of emptiness, of nothingness—the loss of individuality. This nothingness is, of course, the perspective of ego-consciousness. By this it is understood that the ego itself is a differentiated and structured actualization of the Self. Ego-consciousness, in this sense, is always a fabrication of Self-alienation since ego-consciousness does not completely coincide with one's real nature or the totality of the Self. Yet, movement toward the self is the life instinct which will assert itself again and again.

The Collective Unconscious

Jung used the collective unconscious to represent the a priori characteristics of human nature. His development of this particular concept was important inasmuch as the understanding of psychological phenomena is largely seen in terms of ego psychology which tends to understand unconsciousness as derived from consciousness as a personal (ego-conscious) subjectivity.

The distinction between the notion of personal consciousness and collective consciousness is rather important in Jung's analysis. Personal consciousness is made up of present sense-awareness of internal and external objects, and of apparently past objects, all of which are unified within a changing and plastic ego-complex. Consciousness is that relatively small aspect of the total psyche which is related to individuality. That is, Jung understood consciousness as the connectedness of psychic contents to the ego inasmuch as the ego senses them. Collective consciousness means the dominant Weltanschauung expressed in the accepted beliefs, attitudes, prejudices, and dogmas of a particular society or group. Personal unconscious includes events or experiences which have been either repressed or forgotten; psychic elements which are not compatible with conscious attitudes are, therefore, unconscious due to moral, intellectual or aesthetic considerations; thoughts and feelings which have not reached consciousness; and latent functions of the psyche which have not been consciously evolved. Jung's notion of the collective unconscious points to something beyond the ego-complex—beyond the personal unconscious.

Jung used the concept of the collective unconscious which contained

the archetypes of perception and apprehension, which
are necessary a priori determinants of all psychic
processes . . . the instincts and the archetypes together
form the "collective unconscious" . . . it is not made up
of individual or more or less unique contents but of
those which are universal and of regular occurrence . . .
which [have] nothing to do with individuality.[49]

This conceptualization assumes the social nature of human beings to be a
priori. Society is latent in every individual. First comes the individual,
then society. Jung considered the deeper layers of the collective
unconscious to be primarily social.[50] He assumes humans to be herd
animals as has been mentioned earlier. Through these deeper layers of
the collective unconscious arises individualization.[51] The archetypes and
complexes of the collective unconscious are psychic field configurations
and the collective unconscious acts autonomously of the intentionality of
ego-consciousness. It is only when the collective unconscious is viewed
symbolically rather than only rationally that an interaction can be
understood as existing with the discriminating conscious mind. This
relationship can best be understood as complementary in nature since it
balances lop-sided characteristics of ego-consciousness. The Self, as
elaborated earlier, is the totality symbol which is beyond and yet lends
meaning to the conscious and unconscious activities. Jung stresses the
individuation tendency which is the pull toward the Self despite one's
conscious intentions. The collective unconscious, as well, functions
autonomously of the conscious intentions of the ego. It represents the
ancient layers of psychic evolution, in a manner of speaking, which are
dynamic, yet unifying patterns. Jung maintains that ego-consciousness
must continually relate to the unconscious. Not only one's conscious
desires, but the requirements of inner unconscious configurations must be
considered.

Our consciousness does not create itself—it wells up
from unknown depths. In childhood it awakens gradually, and all through life it wakes each morning out of
the depths of sleep from an unconscious condition.[52]

Conscious grows out of an unconscious psyche which
goes on functioning together with it or even in spite of
it. Although there are numerous cases of conscious
contents becoming unconscious again (through being
repressed, for instance) the unconscious as a whole is far
from being a mere remnant of consciousness. Or are the
psychic functions of animals remnants of consciousness?
. . . There is little hope of our finding in the
unconscious an order equivalent to that of the ego.[53]

The archetypes and complexes of the collective unconscious, although
they are societal symbols, are manifested through individuals. That is,
individual consciousness separates itself and emerges from the common
background upon which all individuals dance.[54]

56

Jung pursued the idea that there are universal predispositions to human beings. That is, there are patterns which unfold, so to speak, if no accident interferes in the process. For example, an infant will develop into a child into an adult both physically and mentally. Unconscious function viewed in this light contains the mystery of what is attempting to unfold rather than what is hidden as in the notion of repression.[55] Jung felt that one must go beyond the instincts, sexuality, self-preservation, the power drive and the like because they could not account for the beauty, creativity, and love of the human psyche. In this sense "the unconscious" may be a misleading term as Jung himself acknowledged. It may be that the notion of psyche without modifiers is a more helpful way of viewing the unfolding flow. Progoff notes that

> . . . the psyche is a unitary principle in human life. It is not conscious as opposed to unconscious; neither is it unconscious as opposed to conscious. It is both together. . . . The task of depth psychology is to enter into the psyche in such a way that it touches both its unknowing and its wisdom, linking consciousness and what has been called the unconscious in an integral unity that achieves a fuller development of personality.[56]

To summarize, the concept of unconsciousness is best viewed symbolically. Its meaning is unknown—it is a metaphor. Used otherwise, unconsciousness is merely a contradiction in terms. The attempt to close off the mysterious elements of the life of a human being, by speaking of personality or ego consciousness as the continuity or core of an individual, is an inversion of the Self symbol. That is, a symbol of faith, the Self, has been objectified, or inverted, it has been rationalized. The symbol of the Self as an inversion is an object of experience and is studied as such by rationalistic social scientists whose concern with methodologies (means) of a rationalistic type are, in turn, related to uniformity or standardization (which can become at first a goal, and then a means, and then a goal, and so forth through infinity). The illusion is obtained through the reification of the Self. Ego-consciousness has no meaning in and of itself. The illusion of meaning is created through the concretization of symbol. This is, one might say, an act of bad faith.

Anxiety, Uncertainty, and Fear of Death

Anxiety is essentially the state of ignorance which prevails when one becomes so hardened in his or her ego-conscious attitudes that relation to the transcendent ground symbol of Self is sundered. As it is sundered, one is broken away from the dimensions of life itself with a corresponding loss of orientation. This loss of orientation characterized rationalistic scholarship and mass movements. The pattern of ego-consciousness is, of course, always somewhat at odds with the Self. "When the ego is barred from achieving the task it has set for itself, through the intervention of passion, impotence, pain or death, it must

57

realize that it is not the supreme directing force in the human personality."57

The assimilation of the Self into ego-consciousness is the factor responsible for the inflated view of self which leads to anxiety. Anxiety is not the nature of life itself, but rather the nature of being split off from unconsciousness and the Self. It is the Nietschean "birth of tragedy." Anxiety is the correspondent of rigid identification with ego-consciousness. Anxiety occurs when existence is not experienced symbolically as a mystery beyond the knowing capacity of ego-consciousness. Fear of death emerges as the life instinct is repressed, when the attitude toward the unfolding of life is hardened in an attempt to make life and the world "concrete." Likewise the world, under such circumstances, can be overwhelming since the ego is under the continual intensive threat of being dissolved by the uncertainty and unreliability of a world which cannot be controlled or dominated from the perspective of ego-consciousness in any case. Physical death, thus, is the quintessential limitation of ego-consciousness. Yet, the goal of life is death, and the attitude toward death possessed by one is of great importance and is significant to this discussion. Jung observes that:

> Many young people have at bottom a panic fear of life (though at the same time they intensely desire it), and an even greater number of the ageing have the same fear of death. Indeed, I have known those people who most feared life when they were young to suffer later just as much from the fear of death. . . . Just as, earlier, fear was a deterrent to life, so now it stands in the way of death. We may even admit that fear of life held us back on the upward slope, but just because of this delay we claim all the more right to hold fast to the summit we have now reached. . . . Natural life is the nourishing soil of the soul. Anyone who fails to go along with life remains suspended, stiff and rigid in mid-air. . . . They withdraw from the life-process, at least psychologically, and consequently remain fixed like nostalgic pillars of salt, with vivid recollections of youth but no living relation to the present. . . . The negation of life's fulfillment is synonymous with the refusal to accept its ending. Both mean not wanting to live, and not wanting to live is identical with not wanting to die. Waxing and waning make one curve.58

As has been stated, the unconscious factors are not just psychological, but rather reside in the entire constellation of relationships an individual has with other individuals, and, from the point of view of those interested in politics and social phenomena, in the institutions by which many of these relationships are defined. These rules of the game found within cultures and groups, formal and informal, include language, law, status, role, identity, politics, philosophy and religion. The entire sociopolitical constellation presents ego-consciousness with a conception of itself. When one takes the perspective of difference, of identification with ego-consciousness, one is confronted with change and difference.

The anxiety occasioned by this situation, characterized by contradiction and uncertainty, leads to an array of means to find relief: rigidity, alienation, identification with authority, participation in mass political movements, and religious fanaticism to name a few. These attempts to diminish anxiety fail, since they represent a continuation of that which has created the double-bind in the first place and are, in a certain sense, attempts to "play tricks" upon oneself. Anxiety arises from a basic double-bind involving the fear of death and the fear of life. However, what often hinders the social scientist from pointing out these conflicts and attempting a resolution of them—especially where the contradictions are between an individual, on the one hand, and political institutions on the other—is the social scientist's role. The social scientist represents an institution, and works to establish institutions and uses methods which have little to do with the lives of people. Lest this argument be misunderstood, this does not mean that social scientists should work for the destruction of institutions, that there should be a loss of traditional designs, or that empirical study should be abandoned. It does, however, mean seeing through these patterns rather than coming into identification with them, keeping them in perspective; achieving an integration of consciousness and unconsciousness.

Anxiety is the fear of death repressed. A life which is dominated by rationality and order as the prevalent values, is a life dominated by survival, in which one more and more gives in to the needs of highly bureaucratized, mechanical organizations in the name of utility, necessity, and efficiency. Life becomes overwhelmed with rationality, order, method, and technique rather than being expressed with reason. Fear of death does not only refer to the ceasing of physically vital functions since there is no absolute distinction to be made between the psychic and physical except through the slicing of our analytic knives. Fear of death refers, at once, to the apparent destruction of personal identity, threat to ego-consciousness, or the fear of being unloved.[59] Viewed from another perspective, unconscious elements represent the fear of death to the conscious ego for they are seemingly destructive to the apparent security of the conscious sense of identity. When fear of death is repressed, it is projected by the individual. Uncertainty, the nonrational, and nonorder become objects of fear relating to the death of definition and identity as a person erroneously assumes he or she is an independent agent from the perspective of ego-consciousness and bears the consequences of that illusion.

Work in the United States, as an example, is tainted with fear of death, because in order to survive one must work, and thus survival becomes the great necessity. Survival, psychologically, is the attempt to reach that which is always receding and eluding us. This is reflected in the popular desire to "make it." Despite this orientation, one never actually does "make it," for "making it" and survival are connected in a tautological Weltanschauung. Work does not fulfill some instinctual need either, and Herbert Marcuse has remarked that "to link performance on assembly lines, in office and shops with instinctual need is to glorify dehumanization as pleasure."[60] It can be maintained, for that matter, that work is largely a socially constructed activity in relation to the ideology of social control. In any event, there is no evidence to indicate that people are innately disposed to the assembly line.

Fear of death and fear of life are synonomous, and the quest for survival, which may be socially manifested in the phenomena of achievement, status, prestige, alienation, or identification with authority, is a vicious circle. The following sections will explore the political consequences of fear of death which arise as life is repressed. "It is sufficiently obvious," notes Jung,

> that life, like any other process has a beginning and an end and that every beginning is also the beginning of the end . . . every process is a phenomenon of energy, and . . . all energy can proceed only from the tension of opposites.[61]

The view expressed in this essay is that the interplay of life and death is a fundamental expression of psychic complements, and consequently underlies the form of social and political activity.

The inevitable alienation and disillusionment, or conversely--the identification with authority, which occur when the perspectives of ego-consciousness do not coincide with reality, are manifestations of the fear of death. Of course, how could the picture of reality known in terms of ego-consciousness ever be anything but transient? Again, this is analogous to saying that the part can comprehend the whole. Indeed, one can, however, spend a large amount of energy in patching up the leaks in one's life by building defenses of character, by building up one's persona. Revolution is a phenomenon which is a response, for example, that occurs when people simply do not believe the categorical magic, the character defenses, the persona, the prevalent state order any longer.[62] At the level of the individual, the notion that one can be "in control," is a construct of ego-consciousness itself. To control one's life also means to control one's death, and this, of course, is precisely the problem: one does not control death, and, therefore, does not control life either. This unpleasant discovery is largely covered up through our rationalized and, therefore, standardized, social and political denials of reality. However, insofar as this is true for an individual, he or she lives largely on the plane of projection.

This takes one to the essentials of power--a central concept in the study of politics. Primarily power is a magical or shamanistic phenomenon ultimately having to do with seeming control over life and death--the manipulation of phenomenal reality. To identify with the second-order categories which seem to give control is to engage in immortalization. From the point of view of those who do magic, power can be the proficiency to transform living human beings into things--into

60

cadavers; into a set of behaviors; and, into rational mechanical and moral units. The arrogance, or ego-inflation, which suggests that everything can be grasped is satisfied through the power of dominance or, conversely, through the power of submission—materialistic love. Thus it is that the study of politics is always to some extent the study of the rational ego and the hubris and nemesis of power.

In this, the problem of death is ignored. This is no small matter, as Jung warns:

> Just as man, as a social being, cannot in the long run exist without a tie to the community, so the individual will never find the real justification for his existence, and his own spiritual and moral autonomy, anywhere except in an extramundane principle capable of relativizing the overpowering influence of external factors. . . . Merely intellectual or even moral insight into the stultification and moral irresponsibility of the mass man is a negative recognition only and amounts to not much more than a wavering on the road to the atomization of the individual.[63]

The murder of metaphysical questions through rationalist theory, for example, substitutes a world of second-order expressions, of vital lies, for the extramundane. Since the extramundane ground is the source of order in a human being as well as in political society, disorder attends the "ordering" of the world through ego-consciousness alone. The loss of perspective, through the reification of the rational, permeates existence with the denial of death and with the denial of life. The consequences for the individual, for social scientific understanding, and for politics is large, for an image of the world slowly has emerged in which the ever epiphenomenal individual does not participate, but is steadily suffocated by the collective mass, engaging in immortalizing action with which he is surrounded like a shroud. Such is the shadow life of the herd and its counterpart, rapacious individualism. This represents the sublimation of politics and a corresponding crisis of authority of unprecedented magnitude.

Notes for Chapter III

[1]C. G. Jung. Psychology and Religion: West and East, Bollingen Series XX, Collected Works, vol. 11 (Princeton: Princeton University Press, 1969), p. 417.

[2]T. S. Eliot, "Little Gidding," in Four Quartets (New York: Harcourt, Brace & World, 1943), p. 59.

[3]C. G. Jung, A Commentary on The Secret of the Golden Flower, translated and explained by Richard Wilhelm (New York: Harcourt, Brace & World, 1965), p. 83.

[4]Jung, Psychology and Religion, par. 307.

[5]Jung, Psychological Types, p. 602.

[6]See: Erich Neumann, The Origins and History of Consciousness (Princeton: Princeton University Press, 1965), and Joseph Campbell, Hero with a Thousand Faces (New York: World Publishing, 1949).

[7]Jung, The Structure and Dynamics of the Psyche, p. 185.

[8]"Thinking" is a category of consciousness; thinking channelizes or filters reality into dualistic patterns: subject-function-object. All social theory contains these dualisms, although some theorists choose to repress half of the duality in order to see objectively or rationally. A type of academic authoritarianism is a product of this loss of relation to the transcendent when there is a constant reference to the externality of what others have thought and written without conscious reference to the theorist's own experiencing and thus to the theorist's own unconscious.

[9]Jung, The Undiscovered Self, p. 37.

[10]See: Erich Fromm, "Psychoanalysis and Zen Buddhism," in Erich Fromm, D. T. Suzuki and Richard DeMartino, Zen Buddhism and Psychoanalysis (New York: Harper & Row, 1960). Fromm remarks that:

> Most of human history (with the exception of some primitive societies) is characterized by the fact that a small minority has ruled over and exploited the majority of its fellows. In order to so, the minority has usually used force, but force is not enough. In the long run, the majority has had to accept its own exploitation voluntarily—and this is only possible if its mind has been filled with all sorts of lies and fictions, justifying and explaining its acceptances of the minority's rule . . .

most of what is in our consciousness is "false consciousness" and . . . it is essentially society that fills us with these fictions and unreal notions. (p. 98)

[11]Ira Progoff, Jung's Psychology and Its Social Meaning, 2nd ed. (New York: Julian Press, 1969), p. 204.

[12]Roderick A. Bell and David Edwards, American Government: The Facts Reorganized (Morristown, N.J.: General Learning Press, 1974), p. 215. It was Professor Bell who initially aroused my interest in the work of C. G. Jung.

[13]William Kennedy, "The American Unconscious," unpublished paper delivered to the C. G. Jung Foundation, New York City, 1973, p. 32.

[14]Violet S. DeLaszlo, ed., Psyche and Symbol: A Selection from the Writings of C. G. Jung (New York: Doubleday & Co., 1958), p. 8.

[15]Ibid., p. 8.

[16]C. G. Jung, Mysterium Coniunctionis, Bollingen Series X, Collected Works, vol. 14 (Princeton: Princeton University Press, 1965), par. 129, fn. 66.

[17]Jung, Aion, p. 32.

[18]Ibid., p. 33.

[19]C. G. Jung, Memories, Dreams, and Reflections (New York: Vintage Books, 1963), pp. 348-349.

[20]Kafka has provided us with a literary description:

> It was very early in the morning, the streets clean and deserted, I was on my way to the station. As I compared the tower clock with my watch I realized it was much later than I had thought and that I had to hurry; the shock of this discovery made me feel uncertain of the way, I wasn't very well acquainted with the town as yet; fortunately, there was a policeman at hand. I ran to him and breathlessly asked him the way. He smiled and said: "You asking me the way?" "Yes," I said, "since I can't find it myself." "Give it up! Give it up!" said he, and turned with a sudden jerk, like someone who wants to be alone with his laughter.

Franz Kafka, Description of a Struggle (New York: Schocken Books, 1958).

[21]Jung, Mysterium Coniunctionis, p. 226.

[22]Jung, Aion, pp. 23-24.

[23]Ibid., p. 24.

[24]Jung, The Undiscovered Self, p. 22.

[25]Ibid., p. 23.

[26]Ibid., p. 26, emphasis mine.

[27]Jung repeatedly refers to the experience of Nazi Germany and the sway that Hitler held over the German people in terms of the above. See Jung's "Essay on Contemporary Events," in vol. 10, pt. III, of his collected works.

[28]William C. Kvaraceus et al., Negro Self-Concept (New York: McGraw-Hill, 1965), p. 15.

[29]Jung, Analytical Psychology: Its Theory and Practice, p. 8.

[30]Jung, Aion, p. 33.

[31]Jung, The Undiscovered Self, p. 68.

[32]Ibid., p. 67.

[33]Jung, Aion, p. 4.

[34]Ibid., p. 3.

[35]Jung, The Structure and Dynamics of the Psyche, p. 323.

[36]Jung, Aion, p. 5.

[37]Jung, Mysterium Coniunctionis, par. 129.

[38]This may seem to be an uninteresting point; however, it must be pointed out that this is a fundamental difference between Jung and the psychology of Freud, for example, which places the ego in the central position.

[39]See: Jung, Aion, pp. 3ff.

[40]Otto Rank was quite concerned with this particular dilemma. See: Otto Rank, The Trauma of Birth (New York: Harper & Row, 1973).

[41]See: Alfred Adler, The Practice and Theory of Individual Psychology, trans. P. Radin (Paterson, N.J.: Littlefield, Adams, 1959).

[42]See: M. Esther Harding, The "I" and the "Not-I," Bollingen Series 79 (New York: Pantheon Books, Random House, 1965).

[43]June Singer, Boundaries of the Soul: The Practice of Jung's Psychology (New York: Doubleday & Co., 1972), p. 244.

[44]Ibid., p. 247.

[45]Jung, Two Essays on Analytical Psychology, p. 209.

[46]Ibid., p. 210.

[47]C. G. Jung, Modern Man in Search of a Soul (New York: Harcourt, Brace & World, 1933), pp. 40-41. For example, Freud writes in Civilization and is Discontents: "The primitive, savage, and evil impulses of mankind have not vanished in any individual, but continue their existence in a repressed state . . . and . . . they wait for opportunities to display their activity." And in Psychoanalysis and Faith: Dialogues with the Reverend Oskar Pfister: "I have found little that is 'good' about human beings on the whole. In my experience most of them are trash, no matter whether they publicly subscribe to this or that ethical doctrine or to none at all. . . . If we are able to talk of ethics, I subscribe to a high ideal from which most of the human beings I have come across depart most lamentably" (pp. 61-62).

[48]C. G. Jung, Uber die Energetic der Seele und Andere Psychologische Abhandlungen (Zurich: Rascher, 1928), p. 158, quoted in Singer, Boundaries of the Soul, p. 202.

[49]Jung, The Structure and Dynamics of the Psyche, pp. 133-134.

[50]See: Lucien Levy-Bruhl, How Natives Think, trans. L. A. Clare (New York, 1926); and Lucien Levy-Bruhl, The "Soul" of the Primitive, trans. L. A. Clare (New York). The undifferentiated psyche was understood by Levy-Bruhl who referred to it as participation mystique evident among "primitive" peoples.

[51]See: Progoff, Jung's Psychology and Its Social Meaning, pp. 163-164.

[52]Jung, Psychology and Religion, par. 935.

[53]C. G. Jung, The Archetypes and the Collective Unconscious, 2nd ed., Bollingen Series XX, Collected Works, vol. 9, pt. I (Princeton: Princeton University Press, 1969), p. 281.

[54]The unfolding of the psyche can be likened to the chrysalis, the pupal stage, being transformed into a butterfly. Psyche, in fact, is the Greek representation for butterfly.

[55]Ira Progoff follows the historical development of the unconscious from Freud to Jung. See: Ira Progoff, The Death and Rebirth of Psychology (New York: Julian Press, 1956).

[56]Ira Progoff, The Symbolic and the Real (New York: McGraw-Hill, 1963), p. 74.

[57]Singer, Boundaries of the Soul, p. 240.

[58]Jung, The Structure and Dynamics of the Psyche, pp. 405-407, emphasis mine.

[59]Karl Menninger, The Vital Balance (New York: Viking Press, 1967). Menninger writes:

> The ego faces the various threats of actual and fantasied world destruction, internal demolition and disorganization. These threats relate in part, perhaps, to existential anxiety and the fear of death, but perhaps even more to the fear of being unloved or unlovable. (p. 258)

The existential anxiety to which Menninger refers is the result of a sort of dead living. The fear of being unlovable is actually the fear of death, or, if you will, the fear of life. The source of love is within the individual, although it may come "through" another person.

[60]Herbert Marcuse, Eros and Civilization (Boston: Beacon Press, 1955), p. 221.

[61]Jung, Two Essays on Analytical Psychology, p. 29.

[62]See: Eric Voegelin, From Enlightenment to Revolution (Durham, N.C.: Duke University Press, 1975).

[63]Jung, The Undiscovered Self, p. 34, emphasis mine.

CHAPTER IV

POLITICS AND THE FEAR OF DEATH:
THE CRISIS OF AUTHORITY

In this world, what is the greatest terror?
The fear of death.
                                          - Shankara

What man shall live and not see death?
                                     - Psalms 89:49

The fear of death is the symbol of the growing deterioration of
consciousness due to the separation of consciousness and the unconscious.
The fear of death is the shadow which arises as the unconscious is
devalued through its assimilation to consciousness, manifested in second-
order expressions of human nature, in an overdifferentiated attempt to
defend the dream world—to deny the unconscious.   The decay of
consciousness occurs in two ways: first, the drive of the individuation
process is withered—the pull toward wholeness is diminished and antro-
phied—while the individual is seduced by a depressive neuroticism, and;
second, the individual is possessed by the megalomania of manic spiritual
inflation.[1]   In the case of the individual, the authority of consciousness
is in crisis.   All of these symptoms are significantly present in our
society.   In the case of society, the value hierarchy with its roots in the
collective unconscious, is in crisis. Thus, fear of death can be seen as the
symbol of decay in both the individual and society.   The individual and
society are permeated by the fear of death and the consequent denial of
death. Anxiety is the companion of this fear, a response to the seeming
death of identity and ego-consciousness which is symbolized by the
nonrational.   The bind is a consequence of the assumption that one is an
independent agent, a perspective of ego-consciousness, deriving in part
from the uncritical acceptance of the prevalent dream world or
objectivated world view, but more fundamentally from the schism
between consciousness and the unconscious which, due to its deteriorating
effect upon consciousness, makes it increasingly difficult to critically see
through the illusory nature of second order realities.

Such a perspective contains the experience of uncertainty as
anxiety, irrationality, and chaos. Society, or the world, has, of course,
always changed.   One need only consult oneself to determine this
empirically. When has the world remained still?   In truth, the world can
be characterized as in flux, changing; and seemingly instable; and
apparently, therefore, anxiety-producing where there is the conscious
attempt to maintain stability and consistency or to prevent disorder and
chaos.   The world itself, however, is not anxiety-producing; it is the

perspective of inflated ego-consciousness, cut off from its nondual ground, which has no lasting order and thus produces its own anxiety and fear. That is, when one becomes solely identified with externals without reference to the transpersonal, one is at the mercy of the world. The projections become difficult to withdraw since they carry an emotional charge and seem clearly to be "out there." In our fear we immortalize in order to deny death—to deny the shadow is ours.

The attempts to rationally organize knowledge in order to explain the clearly nonrational aspects of human political activity have, as previously indicated, predominantly taken the form of rationalistic methodologies. This is a form of immortalizing; a response to the fear of death. Returning briefly to the problem of causality, one may say that there are several contexts within which science and, thus, the notion of causality are utilized. What is the cause, and what is the effect? Is there a single cause or a single effect? Is there an invariable association? How does one know that the cause is distinct from the effect, and so forth? In a certain sense, with regard to most of the applications in the social sciences, if one wants to say that there is causality, or probable cause, in a particular theory in some manner or another, one implies law and order. In other words, there is a lawful universe to the extent that it can be believed—to the extent that it is immortal. The reification of science as dogma lends additional strength to the situation. Paradoxically, the psychological aim of scientific and technical efforts to discover the meaning of things, and therefore achieve immortality, is, on the one hand, thwarted since existence within ego-consciousness as well as within the nation, state and among nations remains a contention between life and death, and on the other hand, is merely an attempt to restore what has been described as "a golden age of exact boundaries, an age in which men allegedly knew exactly where they stood."[2] This amounts to an ineffective renunciation of death, but it does not decrease the incredible vitality of ideological, ecclesiastic, or sectarian dogma directed toward a "solution" which has the effect of unifying us all in a circus of the mad.

The western world is characterized historically by Erich Neumann as having come to a crisis in the development of consciousness. The crisis is characterized by the separation of consciousness and the unconscious which "has degenerated into a schism and thus precipitated a psychic crisis whose catastrophic effects are reflected in contemporary history."[3] Since symbols are the link between consciousness and the depths of the unconscious, the nature of the symbol is to set the two in dialectical relationship. The degradation of symbols leads to the disruption of healthy psychic functioning—there is no longer a compensatory flow between the transpersonal and the mundane. Where this occurs, says Neumann, "there is only deadness: dead knowledge, dead facts, meaningless data, disconnected, lifeless details, and dead relationships."[4] When this degradation of symbols occurs, the individual is faced with a difficulty. What are, in fact, systemic problems, are apt to be regarded as personal due to the identification through the persona with an artificially created external and second-order world of ideals with the opposite qualities being thrown into the shadow which then emerge in neurotic form.[5] Jung comments, in what amounts to a "political theory" of the unconscious, that:

> Neurosis is intimately bound up with the problem of our time and really represents an unsuccessful attempt on the part of the individual to solve the general problem in his own person. Neurosis is self-division. In most people the cause of the division is that the conscious mind wants to hang on to its moral ideal, while the unconscious strives after its—in the contemporary sense— unmoral ideal which the conscious mind tries to deny.[6]

As discussed previously, there may be several bases or perspectives from which this "political" problem may be elaborated. Certainly the personal unconscious involves repression of sexual elements as Freud so thoroughly dissertated (Freud's theory, in this sense, mainly addresses the problem of repressed sexuality, although he failed to come to a psychology of the feminine).[7] In Jung's terms a synthesis of the two is formed, and Jung acknowledges that:

> . . . we could easily construct a political theory of neurosis, in so far as the man of today is chiefly excited by political passions to which the "sexual" question was only an insignificant prelude. It may turn out that politics are but the forerunner of a far deeper religious convulsion. Without being aware of it, the neurotic participates in the dominant currents of his age and reflects them in his own conflict.[8]

The political question is one which can be seen from the view of the person who wants power, as well as from the point of view of those willing to confer power.[9] That is, the tyrannical leader needs people to engage in the political—he requires followers. The leader also cloaks his actions with "magical" symbols—national security, the public interest, and so forth, which points to something beyond the leader of which he has knowledge. The relationship between persona and the need for collective as well as individual prestige is analyzed by Jung.

> Masks, as we know, are actually used among primitives in totem ceremonies—for instance, as a means of enhancing or changing the personality. In this way the outstanding individual is apparently removed from the sphere of the collective psyche, and to the degree that he succeeds in identifying himself with his persona, he actually is removed. This removal means magical prestige. One could easily assert that the impelling motive in his development is the will to power. But that would be to forget that the building up of prestige is always a product of collective compromise: not only must there be one who wants prestige, there must also be a public seeking somebody on whom to confer

prestige. That being so, it would be incorrect to say
that a man creates prestige for himself out of his
individual will to power; it is on the contrary an
entirely collective affair. Since society as a whole
needs the magically effective figure, it uses this need
of the will to power in the individual, and the will to
submit in the mass, as a vehicle, and thus brings about
the creation of personal prestige. The latter is a
phenomenon which, as the history of political institutions shows, is of the utmost importance for the
comity of nations.[10]

That is not the end of it, however, since the problem of symbols and the
problem of dogma are related. The phenomenon of dogma is largely
viewed by Jung in terms of the assimilation of the unconscious, as a
psychic inflation. Organizational instances of psychic inflation occur
repeatedly. For example, Jung describes

. . . the humorless way in which many men identify
themselves with their business or their titles. The
office I hold is certainly my special activity; but it is
also a collective factor that has come into existence
historically through the cooperation of many people and
whose dignity rests solely on collective approval. When,
therefore, I identify myself with my office or title, I
behave as though I myself were the whole complex of
social factors of which that office consists, or as though
I were not only the bearer of the office, but also and
at the same time the approval of society. I have made
an extraordinary extension of myself and have usurped
qualities which are not in me but outside me. L'etat
c'est moi is the motto for such people.[11]

It is, of course, not unusual to be acquainted with those who have
identified with their persona in terms of their work. These are people
who assume they are more than they really are. For example, any college
professor who really took the fact that students came to class, took
notes, and studied for examinations as an indication that he or she was
necessarily fascinating and became puffed up as a result of the
assumption would be making an error of personal consequence for the
opposite would be submerged in the shadow. The tendency to take our
work too seriously in the sense of psychic inflation no doubt underlies the
dogmatic rigidity with which we cling to the role, to the persona, and to
the title. Fantasy, of course, produces the inflation, not the role itself.

Identification with one's office or one's title is very
attractive indeed, which is precisely why so many men
are nothing more than the decorum accorded to them by
society. In vain would one look for a personality behind
the husk. Underneath all the padding one would find a
very pitiable little creature. That is why the office--or

70

whatever this outer husk may be—is so attractive: it offers easy compensation for personal deficiencies.[12]

Jung points out that these social factors account only for certain instances of psychic inflation. That is, the objective psyche, or the collective unconscious, contains elements which exercise a fascination and cause psychic inflation. There is also the case of possession by the unconscious. The example of the magical prestige acquired by a mana-figure and the relation to the mass can certainly be examined in terms of the German experience with Hitler. It would also be clear that Hitler is not the only example available. As there is an identification with the collective psyche, there is also the tendency to push desires upon other people since

> . . . identity with the collective psyche always brings with it a feeling of universal validity—"godlikeness"—which completely ignores all differences in the personal psyche of his fellows. (The feeling of universal validity comes, of course, from the universality of the collective psyche.) A collective attitude naturally presupposes this same collective psyche in others.[13]

When this occurs, there can be no psychology of difference. Only the collective, the societal, can be maintained under such circumstances, for the conditions for a truly mass culture have been met. As Jung put it in his essay on "The Gifted Child": The levelling down of humanity into a herd . . . must lead sooner or later to a catastrophe. For if all that is distinguished is levelled down, then all orientation is lost and the yearning to be led becomes inevitable."[14] There is no responsibility in individual terms because emphasis is placed upon the social, the uniform, the organization, and mostly upon the mediocre. "Individualism" is mass culture; it is based in the ideology of the mass itself and merely allows the most predatory individuals under the rationalizations of survival of the fittest to exploit their fellow humans. Individualism, in this sense, is the force and fraud necessary to win the race. That is, it bears no authentic relationship to the individual. This individualism is a flight into isolation. Without their own psychic organization, people who are ordered by individualism are victims of the unconscious. They are, observes, Neumann, "at the mercy of a suprapersonal factor—'work,' 'power,' 'money,' or whatever they like to call it—which, in the telling phrase, 'consumes' them and leaves them little or no room as private persons."[15] Often intellectuals have remarked upon the hubris described in Neumann's characterization, but have felt themselves to be apart from such unconscious factors. This essay has pressed the point that social scientists have a vital part, and have participated in the disintegration of consciousness. The social sciences themselves, including psychology, have been formed, in the modern period, by collective ideologies which were external to the individual and did not emanate from self-understanding. This ideological process is very much involved with education itself. "This process," writes Jung, begins in school, continues at the university, and rules all departments in which the State has a hand. . . . And in so far as he (the man of today) is "normally" adapted to his environment, it is true that the greatest infamy on the part of his group will not disturb him, so long as the majority of his fellows steadfastly believe in the exalted morality of their social organization.[16]

For the scholar, overidentification with the university, or with an office or rank, or with a particular methodology, is identification with the collective and is a resort to immortality in precisely the same manner in which the nation-state represents a type of individualized immortality.[17] All of our rationalisms find their origin in irrational ideologies, and finally dogmas, of immortality. The attempt to dominate or control life is founded in Phobos--the fear of death. But to see that, one must not have allowed the living connections to the unconscious to antrophy. "Anyone who wants to educate must himself be educated. . . . The professional man is irretrievably condemned to be competent."[18] The condemned man, in this sense, always faces fear of death. Neumann wryly notes, "the disintegration of personality caused by an idea is no less dangerous than the disintegration caused by empty, personalistic power strivings."[19] The notion that a devoted tinkering with ideas may lead to a reconstructed and better world even, if this "better world" is defined as "coping" or "adapting," is merely a shamanistic enterprise--the schism of consciousness and the unconscious must be first healed within the individual.

The Degradation of Symbols

The evolution of consciousness and its separation from the unconscious has come to a crisis that is, for the time, essentially negative.[20] This crisis underlies other crises in the Western world and in the United States which have allowed some basic problems of political existence in history to become more apparent. An intense transitional period is being experienced. The historical era of the post-World War II period has been marked, in the United States, by permanent war-readiness on a colossal and unprecedented scale. The maintenance of the social and psychological context pertinent to war-readiness, including political institutions, has been legitimated by several military interventions on behalf of "democracy" and/or "national security." During this time, the relationships of the United States to other nations and to its own people have been profoundly affected by the increased bureaucratization of daily life through the policies created by persons with mentalities shaped predominantly by the apparent necessity to perpetuate the military power and economic growth of the nation-state, and various ideologies, to the exclusion of other alternatives.

The period following World War II in the United States can be characterized as involving a decay of political legitimacy, rapid social and political change, electoral instability as evidenced in electoral behavior in the post-war era, the decline of political parties, violence, economic instability, and disorders of multiple varieties. The crisis had become so acute, that by 1974 neither the President nor Vice President of the United States had been actually elected, but rather had acquired office through an appointment process dominated by the prior office holders who had been forced to resign in disgrace amid widespread corruption. By 1980, no president had served a full two terms since Dwight Eisenhower. Neumann's observations are even more pointed:

> Typical and symptomatic of this transitional phenomenon is the state of affairs in America, though the same holds true for practically the whole Western hemisphere. Every conceivable sort of dominant rules the personality, which is a personality only in name. The grotesque fact that murders, brigands, gangsters, thieves, forgers, tyrants, and swindlers, in a guise that deceives nobody, have seized control of collective life is characteristic of our time.[21]

These irrational manifestations have, interestingly enough, occurred at precisely the same time that bureau-cratization and the objectivation of life reached new levels. It only followed that these events of the irrational type lent themselves to questions concerning the analysis of revolution, change, radicalism, the decline of liberalism, violence, and instability; and, the social science literature of the post-World War II period reflects this concern and usually typifies it. That is, once again, the nonrational roots of political behavior were exposed, and political scientists spent considerable energy in attempting rationally to explain, to organize knowledge in manners which would prove to be acceptable in relation to these questions. The crises of the post-World War II world extend, in a certain sense, to science in general, and to the social sciences in particular. The fear and uncertainty of this historical period, bolstered in the post Vietnam War era by economic uncertainty, are preceded, so to speak, by a crisis of consciousness seen systemically as a crisis of authority or of values--a deterioration of the archetypal canon.

Much of the consequent organization of knowledge concerning politics was a reaction to the perceived threat of death and uncertainty inasmuch as the larger implications in such a situation were that one was participating in a culture whose social and psychological boundaries had become ambigious,[22] and whose decline as the premier world power had been steady since World War II.[23] Political scientists, as well as others, sought knowledge with regard to the existential anxiety attendant to this uncertainty and from the threats to conscious, individual and collective identity, and the degradation and dissolution of values whereby social and political integration could be maintained.

The problem is, of course, that when one becomes impressed by the chaos of the twentieth century, the truth for which one searches in order to give meaning to events can no longer be located in the encompassing symbols. Certainly this is the case of the self of the social sciences.

73

When ego-consciousness is inflated, the experience of which the self is a partial actualization is atrophied. The symbols of self and psyche, once they no longer are in relationship to the unconscious, are inverted through ego-consciousness into ideological entities. And, as one might expect, the clamor for the external reinstatement of values has come from religious and political ideologies which elicit a response in the mass which senses the atrophy. Here, only form is important and this is exactly the position of the rational concept of human nature. The ego-consciousness, however, cannot bail itself out of the dilemma, since, as Jung notes, symbols are of awareness itself and cannot be constructed from the outside. Thus, self salvation which has no authentic relation to the transpersonal is actually self-immortalization.

As symbols degrade from the transpersonal experience to doctrine to dogma to speculation and doubt, meaning comes into crisis. Alienation is, thus, a natural concomitant of ego-inflation. There is an estrangement from the unconscious as one becomes identified with ego-consciousness. Symbols of alienation are associated with crises of authority, with the breakdown of personal and social orientation. When the sources of order are not found in the person, fear of death orders life irrationally. When the Self is identified with ego-consciousness, the symbol complexes of fear of life, fear of death, and immortality motivate order and thus become psychological phenomena themselves. Similarly as symbols degrade, or become equivalent to ego-consciousness, thus becoming beliefs and signs rather than true symbols, such inverted symbols become dogma. Dogma, however, is but a step away from doubt in the process of degradation. The degradation process is not seen by the true believer and his beliefs are defended with great vigor against the nonbeliever because he unconsciously senses the precariousness of his dogmatic world. The dogmatic's world is both moribund and potentially deadly. Moribund since he has lost his soul, deadly because the potential possession by the unconscious directs his energies destructively, due to the conscious ignorance of its attempts at compensation. So, while crises are likely to illuminate fundamental problems of political life in history, the rationalisms which attend to the fear of death, as inflated ego-consciousness is personally and collectively threatened, do not bear upon social and political order, but rather lead to social and political authoritarianism and the depotentiation of the individual--a subject of the next chapter of this essay. The loss of reality of one's existence due to the superimposition of the self of ego-consciousness is pathological.

The manner in which one may halt life and history is through the magic of separate systems. This is true of Marxism and Capitalism, both of which are in crisis. Ego-inflation leads one to name or categorize life so as to make it stand still. Life does not remain still. Unfortunately, for ego-consciousness, there is no dialogue possible, no agreement between a symbol and its degraded forms. This being the case, disillusionment and alienation must result since the rationalism will never be the same as reality and it is only a matter of time before the inverted symbol can no longer be believed. Ego-inflation occurs when all human problems are considered to be solvable by ego-consciousness. That is, alienation results from the natural estrangement of reality and the second-order expression of reality created by the hubris of consciousness. It is in this sense that systems are magical categories and are susceptible to manipulation. At this point it is useful to call attention again to Jung's insight, for the State is a magical category.

> The State in particular is turned into a quasi-animate personality from whom everything is expected. In reality it is only a camouflage for those individuals who know how to manipulate it.[24]

The real social and political problem then becomes: are people being led out of contact with reality through the shamanism of manipulating second-order expressions of reality? If the conceptualization of the behavioral self is an appropriate illustration, then the social sciences are magical and alchemistic inasmuch as Self has been transmuted to personality through the over-estimation of the rational mind. This over-rationalizing activity which paradoxically tends to conscious disintegration involves one in Phobos. There is no rational or intellectual control to be had over the nonrational. There is no rational control of death. There is no rational grasp of life. Fear of death is, then, the bizarre complex of attempting to preserve a world of illusion which must be disillusioning time and time again. Rank wrote:

> This is the meaning of the old traditional wisdom that he who sees the truth must die, because the truth is not only a rational comprehension of interpretation of life but includes--must include if it be truth--its irrational forces, which are destroying the very instrument of the truth-seeker.[25]

A major concern to this point has been with the symbol of Self and its degradation and the consequent separation of consciousness and the unconscious. Once a symbol for the unknown and the mysterious becomes represented as the known, then the Orwellian domain of dogma and the doublethink has been entered. This is the world of fear and death. The realm of Phobos holds sway.

Fear of Death

All people experience the apparent tension between fear of life on the one hand, and fear of death on the other. These fears are complementary, however, since life implies death, being implies nonbeing. The problem is acute only as ego-inflation occurs, as one identifies solely with the duality, the life and death of ego-consciousness. The accompanying fear is embedded in ambivalence--in the ignorance of one pole of the duality which in turn results in a running back and forth between the opposite hypostatized poles of a second-order expression. The experience of this fear arises as duality, and is manifested in independence-dependence patterns. The individualist; and the one who seeks the shelter of the herd. Neither understands. From the perspective of independence, an assertive pattern characterized by "individualism" and isolation is developed. As a human being accumulates a seeming control and power over environment and life, an imbalance is created. The imbalance is answered with fear—the feeling of being isolated, detached, and removed from others, with loneliness becoming the pressing reality of existence. This is the fear of life, which represses the compulsion toward achieving authentic independence and gradually a person may shift to the opposite extreme, dependence, creating an imbalance in the contrary direction. Jung referred to this compensatory function of opposites as enantiodromia. The shift to dependence creates an imbalance which corresponds to a fear of being dispossessed of apparent individuality--the fear of death. Fear of life is the fear of separation symbolized by Rank by birth, by leaving the secure undifferentiated environment of the mother's womb. Fear of death is the fear of losing identity, the fear of becoming fused with other people--a fear that is aggravated by the degradation of the Self symbol and is symptomatic of the search for meaning and the clinging to the doctrinaire and the dogmatic eidolons of abstract extremes.[26]

Fear of death is unconscious and remains repressed, manifesting itself, nonetheless, in the individual and his culture. Herman Feifel has observed that:

> Denial and avoidance of the countenance of death characterize much of the American outlook. Life is not comprehended truly or lived fully unless the idea of death is grappled with honestly. This has implications not only for the individual, but for society as well.[27]

Death is mundane, it happens to all of us, and yet our lives are profoundly affected by the denial of death and the subsequent fear of death. The relationships between mental illness and a person's philosophy of life and death, for example, have been articulated by several scholars. The image of death produces a conscious point of view which is possessed of significances for all realms of life: social, political, philosophical, and religious. The price for denying death is undefined anxiety and self-alienation, for consciousness and the unconscious will continue as separate systems. The fear of death pertains to threats to symbolic life as well as physical life. To understand death from only a physical perspective, without regard to psychic life is an error--death is not merely a biological phenomenon. Despite actuarial tables and boundless statistics, death is also an uncontrollable event—we cannot predict when it will occur for an individual, thus it is a symbol for one of the greatest unknowns. It is the greatest shadow. Therefore, one's understanding and point of view concerning death is important during life. In unfolding, the Psyche is in relation to the continual birth-death-rebirth of the conscious view.

Jung maintains that life is an energy process which is teleological, observing that the goal of life is death, but that death often is not viewed as a fulfillment, but rather as the termination of a process. Jung has eloquently spoken to the problem of the fear of death and its conscious denial in attendance to inflated ego-conscious philosophies.

> Naturally we have on hand for every eventuality one or two suitable banalities about life which we occasionally hand out to the other fellow, such as "everyone must die sometime," "one doesn't live forever," etc. But when one is alone and it is night and so dark and still that one hears nothing and sees nothing but the thoughts which add and subtract all the years, and the long row of disagreeable facts which remorselessly indicate how far the hand of the clock has moved forward, and the slow irresistable approach of the wall of darkness which will eventually engulf everything you love, possess, wish, strive and hope for--then all our profundities about life slink off to some undiscoverable hiding place, and fear envelopes the sleepless one like a smothering blanket.[28]

Jung understands fear of death and fear of life as related. Youth is a striving upward, a driving toward goals and high hopes, an assertion of independence; of differentiation. With the attainment of maturity life takes a downward course and a person should prepare himself for death because "the goal no longer lies on the summit, but in the valley where the ascent began."[29] With regard to death, Jung wrote:

> it would seem to be more in accord with the collective psyche of humanity to regard death as the fulfillment of life's meaning and as its goal in the purest sense, instead of a mere meaningless cessation. Anyone who cherishes a rationalistic opinion on this score has isolated himself psychologically and stands opposed to his own basic human nature.[30]

In a certain sense, nothing that occurs is anything more than the primary interruption of "a perpetual state of rest which forever attempts to reestablish itself."[31]

> A young man who does not fight and conquer has missed the best part of his youth, and an old man who does not know how to listen to the secrets of the brooks as they tumble down from the peaks to the valleys, makes no sense; he is a spiritual mummy who is nothing but a rigid relic of the past.[32]

In a culture, such as that of the United States, where enormous attention is paid to youth--to acting, looking and remaining young; where the elderly are shunted aside; and, where death is hidden--coming to understand death is extremely difficult. One might speculate that the incredible amount of governmental activity related to destructive priorities as opposed to creative ones is a singular manifestation of this fear as is the destructive tendency in rationalistic science. Elderly people do not participate in the community in the same manner as youth. Military expenditures are more important than adequate health care. Our elderly are anachronisms from the point of view of the dominant culture, and "senior citizens," from the point of view of governmental agencies. One cannot, in good faith, avoid the analogy of "doing time" in a penal institution, and "killing time" in the latter part of life as an older person—waiting to die. Fear of death underlies our treatment of older persons, and many older persons, in their own fear, continue to act as though they were young warriors, even though such activities are contrary to the realities of their lives, as they will cling rigidly to a system of imagined universal values of the golden age of their youth. A person who, in nonyouthful years rigidly clings to realities defined in the past, is motivated by a fear of death. The clinging to high definition, a failure to take risks or to see alternatives, is related to a fear of life and, thus a fear of death. This is, of course, paradoxical since the young and the old are inexorably related. An idea central to Jung's psychology here is drawn from Heraclitus: "Out of life, comes death, and out of death, life, out of the young the old, and out of the old the young. . . ."[33] Rigidity is a refusal to flow with life as a process and, when one withdraws from this life process, at least in a psychological sense, and faces backward, one hangs on to that which is purely illusory and which bears no relation to the living present. The same is also true of the future. The future is always a symbol. To degrade this symbol to a known is fear of life, and fear of death at once. Yet this is what is happening contemporarily. This inner organizing potential is needed, otherwise one may be overwhelmed. The relation to the nondual ground of Self is necessary to psychic organization.[34] Otherwise one is caught in the collective. It is in this sense that Jung wrote:

> Resistance to the organized mass can be effected only by the man who is as well organized in his individuality as the mass itself. I fully realize that this proposition must sound well-nigh unintelligible to the man of today.[35]

Identification with the inverted Self symbol means one is "putting his own conception of himself in place of his real being," and thus one

> slips imperceptibly into a purely conceptual world where the products of his conscious activity progressively replace reality. . . . In accordance with the prevailing tendency of consciousness to seek the source of all ills in the outside world, the cry goes up for political and social changes which, it is supposed, would automatically solve the much deeper problem of split personality. Hence it is that whenever this demand is fulfilled, political and social conditions arise which bring the same ills back again in altered form[36]

Surely one can see that this is a critical problem for the academic. The seeming solution is merely a perpetuation, then, of the same problem in changed guise. The reduction of anxiety, as a need, is itself a double-bind. That is, one simply becomes anxious about one's anxieties. The stories, however, which are invented and believed to reduce uncertainty can be found among academics as well as nonacademics. There is, in a certain sense, a politics of knowledge which becomes relevant in the context of the crisis of consciousness in terms of the proliferation of overly-differentiated second-order expressions of reality.[37] Knowledge is itself atomized as it is split from understanding giving rise to what becomes an orthodoxy of the over-specialized. What is to pass for knowledge is itself thrown into dispute in the absence of a psychic organizing principle. Ernest Becker writes:

> What most people usually do is to follow one person's ideas and then another's, depending on who looms largest on one's horizon at the time. The one with the deepest voice, the strongest appearance, the most authority and success, is usually the one who gets our momentary allegiance; and we try to pattern our ideals after him. . . . Today we know that people try so hard to win converts for their point of view because it is more than merely an outlook on life: it is an immortality formula.[38]

The trouble is that immortality formulae always fail. Intellectuals, as well, spend a great deal of time trying to be the deepest voice--organizing knowledge, theories, models, points of view, approaches, and so forth in their attempts to attain success as professional social scientists. In actuality a great deal of this introverted work is done to shore up the defenses, not only of the intellectual, but eventually of the many people who can be socialized into accepting either an inflated or deflated ego-conscious notion of themselves as propounded by intellectuals. Within the academic world of the social sciences, the rational-empirical perspective has developed into a form that allows Becker to conclude that:

> Science, after all, is a credo that has attempted to absorb into itself and to deny the fear of life and death; and it is only one more competitor in the spectrum of roles for cosmic heroics. . . . Psychology was born with the breakdown of shared social heroisms. . . .[39]

Rigidity and the Reduction of Anxiety

Identification with the second-order involves one in what Becker refers to as the "causa-sui project." The project is the illusion that one is immortal "because protected by the power of others and of culture."[40] In the Jungian sense, this is the attitude of inflated ego-consciousness, it is a deception which nonetheless proceeds as one constructs the barriers necessary to avoid the problems of fear of death and fear of life. Fear of death and fear of life are fundamental images at the source, so to speak, of human activity. The nature of anxiety, and of accompanying rigidity, is found in the effort to make the world something other than it really is, that is, to attempt to change it to what the world can never be—consistent, accidentless, pure, and free from death. It is rigidity that argues to the contrary. "The conscious mind," observes Jung,

> is characterized by a certain narrowness. . . . We can never hold an image of totality because our consciousness is too narrow . . . the area of consciousness is a restricted field of momentary vision.[41]

It is a fact that ego-consciousness is symbolic even in the narrow sense. It is symbolic because it is identified with a cultural and social world which provides the roles, statuses, rules, and customs within which identification can take place. Each culture works in this way; the difference between cultures is merely in form, for all provide the definition that people seem to need. The failure is not to recognize that the fear of death underlies the rigidity with which one clings to the social, psychological, or political role. "Chance happenings are repellent to the mind that loves order."[42] To let go, or to give it up would seem like a plunge into nothingness, so one lives in Weber's "icy darkness," for the world has become a prison that has been created from within. The social system is a system that provides the structure of roles, statuses, rules, and folkways within which individuals can assume immortality. Since identification with second-order expressions is tautological, one seems to be the cause in and of oneself. Ego-consciousness may be extroverted and directed to the external world of the symbolic action systems. The more strongly the mood of "getting on" socially becomes, the more the persona becomes rigid and an act of "bad faith."[43] "The persona," notes Eleanor Bertine, "must be a function of relation between the inner and outer opposites."[44] However, when the relation is to the external world alone, then rigidity is the result. Bertine continues by way of illustration.

> Group life is so naively complete, and the illusion of ego autonomy is so convincing that he does not in the least know that he is not perfectly free to be himself. He takes on without objective critique reactions of the group and expresses them with as much fervor and conviction as if they were originally his own. He is, however, under compulsion and lives more or less as a puppet, on a lower stage of development than that of the individual autonomy. It is well known that the whole training of a soldier fits him to play his role in a collective attitude. The obedience to command, the hierarchy of officers, all the military regimentation as well as the collective conditions of life tend to minimize the individual for the benefit of the group. . . . Thus the soldier rarely, if ever, experiences the highest test of his individuality, the necessity to stand alone against the opinions of society and to act accordingly.[45]

80

When identification with the persona is rigid and the unconscious is not given its due, the conditions for a sane group life do not exist since the well-being of the individual now seems to rest with externals and there must be a "normalizing" of any spirited reaction in favor of a necessary and mediocre persona. Once identified in external, ego-conscious terms there is "always the fear that the individual may do something to make the group congeal against him."[46] The only manner is which the rigidity from adapting to conventionality may be overcome is to take a risk by throwing off the persona and recognizing the fear of death which made its hardness possible. Otherwise group life becomes merely an exercise in uniformity where difference is tolerated only in banalized form, but not in substance.

When the self-image or self-worth of a human being is reduced to only the level of ego-consciousness, then that person will feed on external conceptions because there is only "this world." This "worth" can be fed without limit into immortality. It is a race that is actually never won, although it is not understood as such from the perspective of ego-consciousness. Hobbes was an example of this sort of ignorance: "This race we must suppose to have no other goal, no other garland, but being foremost." In the race "continually to be outgone is misery. Continually to outgo the next is felicity. And to forsake the course, is to die."[47] Fear of death is the nemesis of the hubris of consciousness. In the integrated psyche, death, as a negative, has meaning, but in the disintegrated psyche, death is neurotic and a danger to the individual and society for it is unbridled and nihilistic. When rigidity occurs, the presence of ambiguity, change and paradox--life as it actually is--results in anxiety. The rigidity is in terms of the second-order expression of experience and, as such, is an attempt to stop a world which will not actually stop. Inasmuch as eternal, societal formulae are the deciding elements in determining how one will deal with the question of death, the only acceptable solutions will be in the external capacity of inflated ego-consciousness, and hence will be failures, merely stop-gap measures in a race which can never be won since we all are dead from the start and the race is without end. The effort to control death through dependence upon standardized social and political meanings covers up the fear of death and results in its continuation. Then there is the neurotic collective fear of subversion--that the standardized meaning will be subverted, and death will no longer be under control.

The attitudes of the persona always mask inner life and are, therefore, secret neuroses. The hardening of persona provides the seeming security absent in the world. The persona becomes a defense against ambiguity and paradox which, in turn, sees the emergence of the projected shadow which subjects the individual to possession in terms of collective consciousness as fear permeates life. Fear of death involves one in the narrowing down--the avoidance of thought or perception--or, on the other hand, gives one a driven quality as though it could all be solved through ego-consciousness. There is no secure answer in that plane, to life. The building of rigidity, of secure answers, of dogma, is to avoid the fear of death or the fear of life. This is accomplished by the creation of a "self-image" or "self-concept" that will seemingly grant a feeling of worth, by engaging in "consciousness raising" with its ideological under-pinings, or in any one of hundreds of popular therapies designed ostensibly "to make things all right." What, in fact, occurs is the attempt to control death, and when this is carried too far it results in ego-inflation. The second-order within which the identification takes place is illusory, hence the whole notion of human persona also takes on a phantasmic coloring. The over-identification with ego-consciousness takes one further away from the Self, so it would seem, and merely increases anxiety since the circumstances within which one is now involved is a double bind.

> We enter symbiotic relationships in order to get the security we need, in order to get relief from our anxieties, our aloneness and helplessness; but these relationships also bind us, they enslave us even further because they support the lie we have fashioned. So we strain against them in order to become more free. The irony is that we do this straining uncritically, in a struggle within our own armor, as it were; and so we increase our drivenness, the second-hand quality of our struggle for freedom. Even in our flirtations with anxiety we are unconscious of our motives. We seek stress, we push our own limits, but we do it with our screen against despair and not with despair itself. We do it with the stock market, with sports cars, with atomic missiles, with the success ladder in the corpora-tion or the competition in the university. . . . It is fateful and ironic how the lie we need in order to live dooms us to a life that is never really ours.[48]

The wish to be free, in this sense, is the struggle that binds. Once anxiety is met with rigidity and defensiveness, then the fear of death is the feeling of being literally overwhelmed by life. Voegelin has characterized this ego-inflation in the following manner:

> Spiritual impotence destroys the order of the soul. Man is locked up in the prison of his particular existence. It does not, however, destroy the vitality of intellectual operations within the prison.[49]

The only way out of the prison is back out through the way that one got in--that is, rather than grasping, one should let go. The alternative appears to be the continual life of the herd, and possession by unconscious contents. There is, it must be remembered, a natural estrangement between Self and ego-consciousness; and, between reality and the second-order expression of reality from the perspective of the ego. While the seeds of the truth of the matter are to be found within any second-order expression, should one care to look closely enough, often the struggle is continued "within the prison," in approach-avoidance pattern, now regress-ing to the shelter of the herd; now escaping into the alienation of individualism.

Notes for Chapter IV

[1]See: Erich Neumann, The Origins and History of Consciousness. I was aware of the existence of Neumann's work as I wrote the first draft of this essay, but it was not until later, as I went back to revise my work that I read Neumann for the first time with fascination. His essays on "The Balance and Crisis of Consciousness" and "Mass Man and the Phenomena of Recollectivization" were particularly significant for my own work. Having now an acquaintance with Neumann, whose scholarship is far beyond my own, I am grateful to him on at least two counts: first, he has influenced my understanding, and my thinking and its organization in the latter sections of this essay, and; second, and most importantly, in seeing the eloquent parallels in Neumann to my own initial, and somewhat stilted and self-conscious work, I have been encouraged.

[2]Robert Jay Lifton, Boundaries: Psychological Man in Revolution (New York: Random House, 1969), p. xi.

[3]Neumann, The Origins and History of Consciousness, p. 363.

[4]Ibid., p. 373.

[5]The shadow symbol can be seen again and again. A recent example was found in the case of an American Air Force general who, was opposed to the Strategic Arms Limitation Treaty with the Soviet Union unless American military spending was increased, stated ominously: ". . . we must not allow the lengthening shadow of the treaty to soften or hide the very real threat posed by the massive military machine of the Soviet Union" (New York Times, 27 July 1979, p. A-12). The shadow, here, is a reference not only to the rational observation of Soviet power, but also represents the unconscious and darker aspect of American nature as well—the massive military machine of the United States and its malevolent effects upon the character of American life.

[6]Jung, Two Essays on Analytical Psychology, p. 20.

[7]Although Jung's psychology has attracted a disproportionate num- ber of women (who actively work and write) when compared to other psychological schools, the notion of the feminine as used above is meant in its symbolic sense as well as its more literal sense. Jung understood human beings to be possessed of both symbolic principles, while cultural and personal factors serve to repress one side of the masculine-feminine complementarity. A masculine repression of the feminine principle or anima throws it into unconsciousness. Fear of the unconscious anima in collective and historical terms involves the degradation of women. The result is an overly rationalistic world which is rigidly dogmatic in attitude and generally masculine in character. In such a milieu, women are supposed to be the imitators of men. That this problem has long existed

83

in a political sense can be seen in such historical examples as that of Pope Gregory I, Saint Gregory, who declared (circa 600 A.D.) that the Devil was a woman.

[8]Jung, Two Essays on Analytical Psychology, p. 20.

[9]See: John Fowles, The Magus (New York: Dell Publishing, 1965). Fowles includes a discussion of second-order reality in the following dialogue:

> "The human race is unimportant. It is the self that must not be betrayed."
> "I suppose one could say that Hitler didn't betray his self."
> He turned.
> "You are right. He did not. But millions of Germans did betray theirselves. That was the tragedy. Not that one man had the courage to be evil. But that millions had not the courage to be good." (p. 128)

[10]Jung, Two Essays on Analytical Psychology, pp. 150-151.

[11]Ibid., p. 143.

[12]Ibid., p. 145.

[13]Ibid., p. 152.

[14]Jung, Psychological Reflections, p. 149.

[15]Neumann, The Origins and History of Consciousness, p. 391.

[16]Jung, Two Essays on Analytical Psychology, pp. 153-154.

[17]Otto Rank, Beyond Psychology (New York: Dover Publications, 1958).

> education is always an expression of the existing order and remains a willing instrument in the hands of the prevailing type by means of which he imposes his own psychology on the masses. (p. 52)

[18]C. G. Jung, The Development of Personality, Bollingen Series XX, Collected Works, vol. 18 (Princeton: Princeton University Press, 1964/70), pp. 168-169.

[19]Neumann, The Origins and History of Consciousness, p. 392.

[20]For a complete elaboration see: Neumann, The Origins and History of Consciousness.

[21]Ibid., p. 391.

[22]See: Margaret Mead, Culture and Commitment (Garden City: Natural History Press/Doubleday & Co., 1970); and Lifton, Boundaries: Psychological Man in Revolution.

[23]See: Andrew Hacker, The End of the American Era; and, a work, in which civilization is regarded as a decadent phase of a highly developed culture, Oswald Spengler, The Decline of the West (New York: Alfred A. Knopf, 1926-29).

[24]Jung, The Undiscovered Self, p. 26.

[25]Rank, Beyond Psychology, p. 276.

[26]For a literary account of the experience of this type of "abstract arrest" see: Franz Kafka, The Trial (New York: Vintage Books, 1969).

[27]Herman Feifel, The Meaning of Death (New York: McGraw-Hill, 1959), p. xvii.

[28]C. G. Jung, "The Soul and Death," The Structure of Dynamics of the Psyche, p. 405.

[29]Ibid., p. 406.

[30]Ibid., pp. 409-410.

[31]Ibid., p. 406.

[32]Ibid., p. 407.

[33]Joseph Campbell, ed., The Portable Jung (New York: Viking Press, 1971), p. xxvi.

[34]The term "organization" is used metaphorically since the psyche is without a medium.

[35]Jung, The Undiscovered Self, p. 72.

[36]Ibid., p. 93.

[37]The notion of a "politics of knowledge" was first drawn to my attention by Professor Roderick A. Bell in relation to disputes over claims to authority in matters of what was to pass for knowledge. I have used this idea throughout.

[38]Ernest Becker, The Denial of Death (New York: Free Press, 1973), p. 255, emphasis mine.

[39]Ibid., p. 277.

[40]Ibid., p. 187.

[41]Jung, Analytical Psychology: Its Theory and Practice, pp. 7-8.

[42]Jung, Civilization in Transition, p. 113.

[43]Bad faith merely reinforces the illusion, thus thrusting the individual even more profoundly into rigidity and isolation. Bad faith is the attempt at self-deception.

[44]Eleanor Bertine, Jung's Contribution to Our Time (New York: G. P. Putnam's Sons, 1967), p. 127.

[45]Ibid., pp. 211-212.

[46]Ibid., p. 118.

[47]Thomas Hobbes, The Elements of Law, Natural and Politic, ed. Ferdinand Tonnies (2nd ed.; New York: Barnes & Noble, 1969), pt. I, chap. 9, sec. 21.

[48]Becker, The Denial of Death, p. 56.

[49]Eric Voegelin, From Enlightenment to Revolution (Durham, N.C.: Duke University Press, 1975), p. 298.

CHAPTER V

MASS MAN, INDIVIDUALISM, AND NONPARTICIPATION:
THE TYRANNY OF THE UNCONSCIOUS

It is a fact that cannot be denied: the wickedness of
others becomes our own wickedness because it kindles
something evil in our own hearts.[1]

The crisis of culture involves the disintegration of the value
hierarchy. Values become inverted as their archetypal ground is degraded
and lost as a consequence of the split between consciousness and the
unconscious. Dead, empty replacements emerge as the shadow values of
inferior man. Love, fairness, honesty, truth, security, individual, God,
spirit, death are all degraded as their relation to human experience
deteriorates. In their place have slowly come to stand the isms of the
shadow--the ideologies of the dream world of mass man--capitalism,
Marxism, communism, socialism, individualism, materialism, feminism,
chauvinism, and Christianity, to name but a few of the more prevalent
complexes. If the individual does not hear the voice of the unconscious
within himself, then the disintegration of values, around which individuals
could participate in life, represents the loss of the transpersonal.

The death of symbols with their roots in the collective unconscious
leaves behind only lifeless fossils. Vitality is replaced by the doctrinaire
and the dogmatic. The archetypes, as a result, fall into unconsciousness
and are projected into the world in negative and destructive forms where
they will remain until the link to the unconscious is opened and the
archetypes are bound. When the center does not hold, the phenomenal
world falls apart and the Self is lost to the hubris of consciousness which
attempts impotently to solve the problem of the collapse of the hierarchy
of values in which it is unwittingly involved. The separation of
consciousness and the unconscious results in the appearance of two
phenomena which are of interest to the socio-political dimension of this
discussion, and which will constitute the focus of the concluding section
of this essay: first, is the tendency of the individual to seek the shelter
of the herd, the supposed security of the collective mass; that which
Neumann calls, in archetypal language, a "regression to the Great
Mother," and; second, is the "flight to the Great Father," an escape to the
alienation and isolation of individualism.[2]

The occurrence of social and political instability, in part, coincided
with the diminishing of an historical and normative political science,
which valued philosophy; and, the concurrent growth of a rational-
scientific political science beginning in the post World War I period. This
trend in political science was purported to center on the political behavior

87

of individuals while, in fact, a collective ideology, fostered through education, was developing. The understandings which would allow a person to survive systemic changes were not pursued because, after all, inner life could not really be measured, only inferred. Instead, mass education, supported by the rational-scientific tendency, made it relatively impossible to be educated, unless one educated oneself despite the school. Otto Rank observed that,

> just as traditional education aims at the establishment and perpetuation of the existing social order and the psychological type representing it, the individual's self-development tends toward difference, hence, makes for change. In this sense, educational philosophies, no matter how radical their origin, tend to become conservative if the social system which supports them is to endure.[3]

It is in this sense that Hess and Torney can rightfully claim that the primary function, the consequence of socialization, within the primary school is, in the political sense, to introduce children into an authority-compliance system.[4] That is, children are taught to respond to social and political order—to "fit in." This process has not been altogether different at the level of university education either inasmuch as education has become a predominantly hierarchical and over-specialized affair. The more highly specialized university education became, the less possible it was to become a generalist. The paradox of this matter simply was: the more specialized one became in terms of the graduate and professional discipline, the less one, in fact, knew. The greater the differentiation of consciousness, the further one seemed to be from understanding.

Authoritarianism and Education

Bell and Edwards refer to the external coordinating features of bureaucratized education by noting that "this cultural achievement" is such that its awareness "eludes the individual: seen from the 'outside,' the university is the institutionalization of a prodigious amount of knowledge; but the farther 'into' the university one gets, the farther away from all that knowledge he finds himself."[5] The more elaborate the ideology of hierarchical and specialized education becomes, the more latent the spontaneous and nonrational elements within such an ideology become. This, in turn, involves intellectuals in additional rationalizations of the nonrational—of those things which do not fit. Rank writes:

> the different political creeds, educational systems and psychological schools are striving for a supremacy which cannot be established by any absolutistic dogmatism. Each of these ideologies, while claiming to have found the very truth, is actually only expressing temporary needs and desires of one side of human nature, thereby forcing the other frustrated side to assert itself alternately in violent reactions. Hence we have the eternal

cycle of changing ideologies, in the face of which we
still cling to the faith in an absolute solution.[6]

The problem of specialization has yet to be realized in its fullest extent,
for it has bred a type of academic authoritarianism which is pervasive and
yet obscure at the same time. The more highly specialized, the more the
intellectual is deeply mired in the purely conceptual; in speculation about
ideals and abstractions. There are at least two major symptoms of this
syndrome: first, there is a tendency toward the memorization of large
amounts of bibliography which pertain more to schools of thought than to
knowledge. This acquisition of bibliography is then what passes for being
"well-read," but is often a form of obsequiousness. Secondly, is the
dynamic toward the dogmatic upholding of a particular set of ideas, or,
conversely, the grasping at every passing fad within a discipline in order
to "make it" professionally under the guise of "keeping up with the
discipline" or being eclectic. As a result of this rational tendency in
academe, knowledge has passed into an ideological stance characterized
by explanation which, from the view of politics, is a means to transform
life in terms of a particular sociopolitical order. That is, education is
mass education. Education is a regression to the Great Mother.

Ideologies pretend to rationality, while, in actuality, they are
possessed of emotional content since there has to have been an
assimilation of the unconscious to ego-consciousness. As an example, in
speaking to psychology, although other social sciences can be characterized in the same terms, Rank states:

> What we actually find in practice is a variety of
> psychological theories sponsored by different leaders
> who accuse each other of not being scientific without
> realizing that their psychologies, as they have been
> interpreted and used in practice, are in reality ideolo-
> gies representative of certain classes and types.[7]

Inasmuch as university educators, legitimated by the tenets of
scientific rationalism, socialize and condition people in terms of the
ideology of schools of thought and of mass specialized education, they are
engaged in perpetuating their own immortality formulae. That is, people
can be conditioned into accepting inflated ego-conscious notions of self,
justified by the entire weight of expertise and "scientific" authority when,
in fact, such notions of self refer to the overly rationalized nature of
organization within education itself with its purpose of uniformity. The
purpose of rationalistic explanation which reduces the self to a socio-
political unit or an ideal is to actually make people alike, in order to
compare them, to fit them to the speculations, to describe them
collectively, through, as Rank suggests, "an indoctrination of educational,
therapeutic or political ideologies."[8] This trivializes the individual.

The more the individual can be indoctrinated with the triviality of
his psyche, of its worthlessness, the more susceptible to the collective
immortality symbols he becomes as identification with intellectual

ideologies, dominant racial groups, movements, social classes, types, or nations occurs. Rank remarks:

> Herein I see the origin and meaning of warfare and revolutionary struggle, which so far have precipitated the most decisive social changes in history. This dynamic force of change springs from the eternal conflict between man's desire for personal immortality as against biological survival, which is anti-individualistic and can only be attained by a more or less homogeneous group of people. Man's immortality, being naturally universal, that is, the survival of mankind on earth, has been individualized from time immemorial in order that he might maintain his belief in personal immortality. Since this always remains uncertain, man resorted to a collective immortality originally embracing small units, such as the clan or tribe, and eventually extending to the conception of a nation. Hence, nationalism already represents a form of individualized immortality as compared to the survival of mankind in general.[9]

The fear and consequent denial of the unconscious, the unknown, the uncertain, and, ultimately, the fear of death attracts people to the immortality of the collectivity. In the academic world, intellectuals are attracted to the collective immortality of schools of thought, methodologies of uniformity, and ideal speculations for the same reasons. An interesting study, no doubt, could be done with regard to the effect of "publishing or perishing" on the hardening of the mood of survival, and the consequent rigidity and identification with a collective view in a fit of creative individualism, which for the individual scholar may be manifested in his work. From the perspective of politics, "warfare and revolution," notes Rank, "no matter how well rationalized, historically, have their origin in those irrational ideologies of immortality, that is, in the man-made conception of survival; hence, are bound to fail in their attempt to establish supernatural conditions in this world of reality."[10] Revolution must fail in this sense since it only involves the ascendency of another set of rulers, in terms of elites, classes or groups, which are better armed than the previous set of rulers. That is, what is accomplished is a change of power, although not necessarily any improvement for the mass of people. Carl Becker provides the historical example:

> We have been told, as if it were a surprising thing, that in Russia the Revolution has been betrayed. It is in the nature of revolutions to be betrayed, since life and history have an inveterate habit of betraying the ideal aspirations of men. In this sense the liberal-democratic revolution was likewise bound to be betrayed--men were sure to be neither so rational nor so well intentioned as the ideology conceived them to be.[11]

Likewise are our intellectual revolutions also betrayed.

The second-order reality divides itself finally into the categories of good and evil as it pertains to ideology. Invocations of divine power, "God is on our side," "I've got the hard data," are familiar ideologisms. What this really means is that those who are successfully in power become good and, as Rank notes, "Take it upon themselves to make the citizens virtuous. . . ."[12] The crisis of consciousness remains. As long as the ideology of rationalism dominates the social sciences, solutions to problems will fall into two polar categories: first, the individual will be accused of all sorts of inadequacies; and, second, the existing social order will be blamed. "This controversy," remarks Rank, "between hereditary versus environmental causation of human behavior is only a game of hide and seek played by our wishful thinking."[13] Such are the problematics of causation.

The dynamic of social science is to force the individual into standardized expectancies through its rationalistic ideology. The tendency toward uniformity, in this sense, where difference is, in reality, unacceptable, through the bureaucratized nature of education, rationality, or the use of statistical-mathematical methods which deal with ideal averages, is to put one in the position of feeling "compelled to change others according to himself."[14] The seeds of authoritarianism as they exist within the university and the social system are to be found in the fear of death and this need for immortalization. Rank characterizes "such craving for likeness in the face of all the multiform differences . . . ," to originate "in man's need to counteract the negative aspect of individualization, in the last analysis, death, by the most primitive and elemental idea of perpetuation: namely, the immortalizing of one's own self in another resembling it as much as possible."[15] Much scholarship could certainly be characterized as an immortalizing effort in this negative sense; to be professional, to be in the position to perpetuate one's views of the discipline, to continue on after death. In turn, the problem of the student may not be overlooked, for reliance on standardized test scores and grades, the validity of which must be in some doubt at least, have an effect on the nature of undergraduate and graduate study within a discipline. Mathematized evaluations, it can be argued, by way of illustration, merely represent the existing order of things, the rationalistic bias, and do not necessarily bear any relation to the individual development of knowledge and understanding, but rather represent the institutionalized non-ability or ability to play the depotentiated role of student. Thus, there arises the tendency to produce either obsequious or alienated students as well as obsequious or alienated faculty.

The common thread of the previous observations is simply that as life becomes a second-order expression, there arises a need for immortalization due to the fear of death. Immortalization can be expressed either in collectivism or in individualism. The political system, the nation, is an immortality system itself. It provides the definition necessary to immortality from the perspective of politics. This is the illusion of immortality. "The national character," says Jung,

> is an involuntary fate which is imposed upon the individual like a beautiful or ugly body. It is not the will of the individual which conditions the rise or fall of a nation. . . . It is therefore illusory to praise or bless nations, since no one can alter them . . . the "nation" . . . is a personified concept that corresponds in reality only to a specific nuance of the individual psyche. The nation has no life of its own apart from the individual, and is therefore not an end in itself.[16]

The fear of death always involves one deeply in an immortality system. The problem becomes intensified, however, as social and political crises occur since such crises are related to the degradation of symbols and the fading away of meaning--then meaning itself becomes a question. "Grounds of an unusually intense fear of death," Jung mentions,

> are nowadays not far to seek: they are obvious enough, the more so as all life that is senselessly wasted and misdirected means death too. This may account for the unnatural intensification of the fear of death in our time, when life has lost its deeper meaning for so many people, forcing them to exchange the life-preserving rhythm of the aeons for the dread ticking of the clock.[17]

Authoritarian Man

When the psychic organization, so to speak, of an individual is inadequate, when the ego is in a state of inflation, then there is the tendency to regress to identification with the collective, to external situations which can provide the definition for role expectations. Lt. Calley, for example, blamed the army; he did not, and apparently was not able to, do other than what he claimed his military training had taught him to do--and he, in his neuroticism, could maintain, that he did not understand.[18] Authoritarianism, as the notion is used here, has several components: first, there is an association with ignorance--an ignorance of the Self, self-division, and consequent fear of death; second, rigidity and an accompanying reduction in the scope of alternatives available to the individual; third, anxiety, with an increase of dependence characterized also by the emergence of independent characteristics in neurotic form; and, fourth, an identification with authority.

Authoritarianism as ignorance involves the assimilation of the unconscious and results in two seemingly opposite, although complementary, phenomena: rapacious persons who fall into hubris; and, those who are overwhelmed by the feeling of powerlessness. Jung writes in reference to the assimilation of the unconscious that,

92

It produces in some an unmistakeable and often unpleasant increase of self-confidence and conceit: they
are full of themselves, they know everything, they
imagine themselves to be fully informed of everything
concerning their unconscious, and are persuaded that
they understand perfectly everything that comes out of
it. . . . Others on the contrary feel themselves more and
more crushed under the contents of the unconscious,
they lose their self-confidence and abandon themselves
with dull resignation to all the extraordinary things that
the unconscious produces . . . give up all sense of
responsibility, overcome by a sense of the powerlessness
of the ego. . . .[19]

These extremes are possible within the domain of duality as identification
with ego-consciousness occurs. Furthermore, there can be a running back
and forth between the poles of independence and dependence; or
avoidance and approach. The only difference involved, in fact, is that,

One man arrogates collective virtue to himself as his
personal merit, another takes collective vice as his
personal guilt. Both are as illusory as the megalomania
and the inferiority, because the imaginary virtues and
the imaginary wickednesses are simply the moral pair of
opposites contained in the collective psyche. . . .[20]

The ignorance of the unconscious can result in possession by the
collective. This is precisely why masses of people have followed leaders
who are, in Jung's terminology, "mana-personalities." There is a certain
fascination with a personality that wields or holds power, for that person
seems to confer immortality as well. In reality, the fascination has arisen
within the individual, although in the transference magical qualities are
seen in the leader, and the leader may himself be possessed by the
archetypes. The leader, in this sense, is regarded as being able to lift
from the individual the problems of life, and of death—this is the
archetype of the Great Individual, the "revelatory" bearer of the
transpersonal who could be either prophet or madman.[21] The politician
as leader, however, is the individualist who is an appendage of state
power. The politician, as such, has nothing to reveal which would illumine
the relationships necessary for group, as opposed to mass association, life.
His "insight" is empty and transient. This is because the State, of which
the politician is a part, has no interest whatever in advancing or truly
encouraging mutual understanding among people because, first, it is not
clear that such is within the ability of the State and, more importantly,
the more unrelated individuals remain, the more consolidated the State
may become. In this consolidation more power will come to those who
possess the position and resources to manipulate the symbols of the State.

    The individuality of the unconscious is blotted out, and the moral
responsibility which is rightfully that of the individual is replaced by the
policies of the nation-state and may become a form of state slavery.

93

Jung observes that

> every man is, in a certain sense, unconsciously a worse man when he is in society than when acting alone; for he is carried by society and to that extent relieved of his individual responsibility. Any large company composed of wholly admirable persons has the morality and intelligence of an unwieldy, stupid, and violent animal. The bigger the organization, the more unavoidable is its immorality and blind stupidity. . . . Society, by automatically stressing all the collective qualities in its individual representatives, puts a premium on mediocrity, on everything that settles down to vegetate in an easy, irresponsible way.[22]

Persons are dogmatically attracted to the collective symbols out of ignorance, because such identification is necessary to obscure the fear of death and provide the illusions which support the inflation of ego-consciousness. The State, as well as all mass organizations, could not, of course, exist without the phenomena of imitation and conditioning, through which people can be led into identification with the collective. In this manner one may build up a superb persona, but as Jung notes, the "punishment of this [is] the uniformity of . . . minds . . . and unconscious, compulsive bondage to the environment."[23] It is in this sense that Jung has contributed so greatly to the understanding of authoritarianism inasmuch as he regards persona as a mask which "feigns individuality," while in actuality "one is simply acting a role through which the collective psyche speaks."[24]

It is not difficult for a person to project unconscious content onto a leader. This projection gives the necessary prestige to the leader in a symbiotic relation of transference which correspondingly confers apparent immortality on the individual. The projection is, in this sense, an effort aimed at establishing security and meaning in terms of the environment or the leader. The fallacy here is that the anxiety which is to be banished through identification is continued through essentially engaging in a false or second-order world. Negative identification and transference is also possible, and Jung writes, the "negative form of transference in the guise of resistance, dislike, or that endows the other person with great importance from the start."[25] Approach and avoidance, in this sense, are merely the negative and positive sides of the same coin, while ultimately underlying the transference is the fear of death. The transference is the process of immortalizing, so that fear may be removed through the identification with the externalities which seemingly grant perpetuation. The transference then, occasioned by the assimilation of the unconscious, provides the individual with the illusion by which to seemingly secure significance. Unhappily for the individual the illusion will most likely remain an illusion.

Attendant to authoritarianism is rigidity and the reluctance through the narrowing of one's world to face risk or uncertainty--the failure to participate. This means that the more the dependence upon external authority, the less one need engage in one's own decision-making. Fear of death leads one into the immortality paradox, for it is hoped that the uncertainty involved in making personal decisions can be avoided, while any decision, of course, involves a risk--an unknown. The unwillingness to engage in uncertainty freezes one within the collective psyche, for then no participation is possible. Whenever one must decide something, there is not only the problem of choice, but also of doubt and faith. In political terms, the leader or other collective symbols can apparently remove that doubt and uncertainty. In fact, the politicians try to "restore faith," which is nonsense, but if such propaganda is believed, then one may seemingly not have to worry about the manner in which decisions are made, one can fail to participate, although political leaders may still take one to war or subject one to all sorts of incredible risks in the name of national security and the like. But this attempt to reduce anxiety, paradoxically, only serves to intensify the need for certainty and thus further intensifies anxiety. The fact that the country is currently ungovernable is hidden, yet suspected.

Once identification has been in systemic terms, then rewards and punishments are, in turn, also systemic functions. It is the system, the magical category, which then rewards the individual in terms of his or her desires in society. Contrariwise, systemic punishment occurs when the desires are not met.[26] Severe instances of identification with the system in order to reduce the anxiety of systemic punishment have been documented.[27] Jung notes that there are essentially two general ways in which people try negatively to free individuality from the collective psyche: first a "regressive restoration of the persona." As an illustration, Jung writes of the person who takes a risk and fails. Jung states that if

> he goes all to pieces, abjures all further risks, and laboriously tries to patch up his social reputation within the confines of a much more limited personality, doing inferior work with the mentality of a scared child, in a post far below him, then, technically speaking, he will have restored his persona in a regressive way. He will as a result of his fright have slipped back to an earlier phase of his personality; he will have demeaned himself, pretending that he is as he was before the crucial experience, though utterly unable even to think of repeating such a risk. Formerly perhaps he wanted more than he could accomplish; now he does not even dare to attempt what he has it in him to do.[28]

The second method is one which bears relationship to identification with authority itself. In Jung's terms it is "identification with the collective psyche." The implication for the civil religion that is called the State is enormous. This second effort, according to Jung,

> leads to identification with the collective psyche. This would amount to an acceptance of inflation, but now

exalted into a system. That is to say, one would be the fortunate possessor of the great truth which was only waiting to be discovered, of the eschatological knowledge which spells the healing of nations.[29]

This is the condition for the phenomenon of the religious leader and of religious fanaticism which should not be underestimated in our time. The split of consciousness and the unconscious has resulted in the projection of the negative aspects of religion into contemporary life. Religious cults abound. Christian fundamentalism has even entered politics in an organized manner. Islamic fundamentalism has expressed itself abroad in similar, yet more violent fashion. Many of the mass have received the "truth" and are prepared to thrust it upon their neighbors. The historic schism of the psyche must be seen, in phenomenal terms, also as a spiritual crisis. In this circumstance, religious ideologies will emerge as readily as political and social ideologies. In fact, the political battles most likely are the harbingers of only more violent religious upheavals. Mass religious activity is an identification with the collective psyche, and thus the individual is relieved of the courage and discipline needed to probe his own soul for he is sure that he has received "the word," an illusion which is reinforced by the emotionality of mass experience. Religious ideology merely provides the mass man with a transient, but consuming, sense of messianic fervor. The mass will even murder and commit suicide in the pursuit of their "enlightenment." The ideological religions, with their self-righteous attitudes, obscure, for the individual caught in the religious mass, the possible illumination of spirit which comes from the inner search which was and is the heart of all authentic religious experience. The revelatory symbols of religion have, as have other values, also deteriorated in the modern period into doctrine and dogma, into creeds, although this could never be accepted by the true believer who sees doctrine and dogma in "the church," or in "other faiths," but not in his own, even though his own religious ideology provides him with "the four spiritual laws," or some equally banal set of principles.

This is the religious aspect of the hubris of consciousness--a reduction of the spiritual to the mundane--a religious immortality formula. The self-righteous character of religious possession is clearly noticeable. And, in speaking to religious authoritarianism, Jung remarks that:

> This is an identification with the collective psyche that seems altogether more commendable: somebody else has the honour of being a prophet, but also the dangerous responsibility. For one's own part, one is a mere disciple, but nonetheless a joint guardian of the great treasure which the Master has found. One feels the full dignity and burden of such a position, deeming it a solemn duty and a moral necessity to revile others not of a like mind, to enroll proselytes and to hold up a light to the Gentiles, exactly as though one were the prophet oneself.[30]

While this may not seem such an important point in terms of politics, it may be of some worth to reflect on the religious dimensions of warfare which we find manifested in Ireland and the Middle East and of politics in the United States. In the long range, admittedly a speculation, we may currently be viewing the embryonic immortality symbols upon which the future State shall rest.[31]

Ideology is then, in effect, a collection of symbols which have been taken in a doctrinaire sense; but which still contain a vitality of their own. Ideology is itself the unmoral pole which offers the absolute solution to history and life. As a polar type, it always invites the opposition of counter-ideologies. The dominant ideology within a nation-state represents, as a collective symbol, individualized immortality. It is however, on the other hand, rather obvious that what seems to be the prevalent ideology is not accepted by all persons within the body politic. As Singer notes:

> There have always been ways of resisting the attitudes of the establishment, the "collective consciousness." People have not had to look far to find them. In a milieu where intellectual values are overstressed, the non-rational elements of the human personality are forcibly repressed. Still active in the unconscious, they offer up ideas separated and unacceptable to the ruling elements of the society. Then it is that most dissident groups develop, or dissident individuals whose interests and behavior bring to light the formerly unaccepted and hidden aspects of the group's or individuals' nature.[32]

This, the possibility of counter-ideologies, brings us to a discussion of alienation.

Alienation and Mass Man

Alienation is a difficult subject to broach simply because its meaning has been largely lost through the rational utilization of concepts such as: anomie; alienation; rebellion; disillusionment; powerlessness; and, so forth. What these concepts have come to represent in the social sciences is the failure to adapt. Illustratively, alienation, in the behavioral view, is what occurs when the rules of the game which serve to define behavior are confused, weakened, or ineffective. The question of who is to adapt to what is, of course, not raised. A brief perusal of the relevant literature concerning alienation or anomie reveals a whole set of concepts which find their source in rational behavioral functional analysis, generally based in some sort of assumption about equilibrium, among which are: function and dysfunction; breakdown of social or psychological organization (external); breakdown in communication; conflict in goals; role conflict; normative confusion; disruptions in social rankings; a crisis in values; and so forth. It is not the various dimensions of alienation that cause the obscuring, it is rather the behavioral

97

insistence that a failure to adapt has occurred—the insistence that something happens out there, which ignores inner life, producing the basis for a neurotic social science. Once it has been assumed that something has occurred externally, then the questions of how the political system or social system may be manipulated to relieve us of such a crisis arises. Of course, this is not a solution, but a perpetuation of the problem, since creeds, governments, and social science cannot solve what are really spiritual crises. Such "breakdowns" are actually "solved" through essentially mysterious processes which are so personal that they cannot be manipulated or arranged in a fit of social or moral engineering.

It would seem to be quite correct to assert historically that alienation symbols appear to prevail, in various forms, during periods of transitions—that is, when the world no longer seems to make sense. This would be a period in which the symbols that provided the meaning for integration have degraded, have been emptied of their value, and this period is accompanied by the arising of alienation symbols. The symbols of alienation convey the meaning of the world as a prison which one must either change or escape from; or, failing in these, one must fatalistically withdraw because authority provides insufficient meaning with which to identify and one's life on earth is suffering. A judgment that alienation is caused by failure to adapt, in any of the manifold aspects of this rationalization, is the same as saying alienation is caused by alienation which is an absurdity. The failure to adapt is merely the finding of the cause in the effect after the fact. With respect to external solutions, no intentional creation of symbols can occur since they are spontaneous in character and substance, and thus the question of adaption is merely the continuation of the authority symbolisms which exist as attempts to put the world right. It is also the case that utopian symbolisms make their appearance during periods of intense sociopolitical disturbance, and also use alienation as the rationale for changing the world.

Alienation, then, is regarded as a complex of symbolisms which bear correspondence to the attempt not only to reestablish traditional order, but also to reorder in utopian terms. Of course, it would seem that those who are identified with authority will have a greater tendency to support authoritarian policies and resent attacks on authority, while those who identify with alienation symbols will, in their estrangement, possess less of such a tendency, although identification with utopian ideals may be fiercely supported where a meaningful counter-ideology has arisen for an individual. Alienation, paradoxically, underlies authoritarianism in both its traditional and utopian extremes. These forms, as well as over-intellectualized forms, however, can never provide an explanation of alienation since they typify it.

The phenomenon of alienation is very much bound up with the estrangement of ego and Self which is manifested both in individualistic and collective terms. Since the ego is always a partial actualization of Self, the value systems, ideologies, roles, and goals of society which tend to give structure and definition to the ego, are themselves partial—constrained and constraining. When characteristics are developed which do not fit the ideals of the ego, they fall into unconsciousness, into the shadow, and, in turn, are projected onto the world. It is merely a dream to assume that the ego is somehow free and unconnected to the "things" outside and inside from which it has separated itself. The degraded notion of freedom arises from the claim that one creates one's own feelings and thoughts, when, in fact they arise and recede in one's awareness which is itself a mystery. The pattern of ego-consciousness seems, from that perspective, to be at variance with the reality of the Self. In historical perspective, ego conscious notions of reality, always involving some notions of the ideal, are once removed from the reality itself, and thus there is always a natural alienation of the ideological, the idealized, or the conceptual from the process of history since history is itself a symbol and a process of discovery and illumination. In this sense, there is no agreement between a symbol and a degraded symbol even though the language may not vary. Thus the problem of alienation can never be reduced to linguistic analysis.

The second-order is never the same as the reality but is merely the medium. Thus, given the crisis of consciousness in our time, there is always a crisis of authority, so to speak, for the world can never turn out to be the place that is conceived of. The approach side of identification with second-order notions can be seen as identification with authority, while the avoidance side can be viewed as identification with second-order notions which express the meaning of alienation, of disillusionment. In either case, the problem is that there is an inability to participate since there is, in a sense, an abstract arrest of the person. Life, rather than being symbolized as an unfolding process, occurs as a second-order reality of polar types.

The ego-Self alienation corresponds to the collective phenomenon of the breakdown of traditional order. That is, crises of authority occur when the symbols within which persons can locate themselves are no longer meaningful. Politically, when people feel powerless, they may turn to the experience of mass movement. This is, of course, related to the whole process of the degradation of symbols which has been previously discussed. The experience of reality under such circumstances produces not only the symbolization of authority and immortality, but also the related symbols of alienation. Because of the degradation of the Self symbol, one is paradoxically also withdrawn from existence in time. The world is sensed to be the cause of our alienation from the world in which we should belong. Alienation symbols arising in circumstances of both individual and collective disorder are partial actualizations which may, in turn, become doctrinaire second-order expressions of ideology providing the "reasons" for the need to create heaven on earth or to withdraw from life.

Alienation, in effect, is a mood of existence with the consequence that we become strangers in a place that is itself strange. The individual and the world become hypostatized. The individual has retreated into individualism and has effectively isolated himself. This is neurosis to Jung's mind, since there has now been an individual identification with what is actually systemic, which requires the individual to close himself or herself off, to fail to participate. Likewise, in terms of political action, there is diminishing of participation among both the alienated and the authoritarian since both are identified, respectively, with systemic punishment and systemic reward and the basis for group participation as contrasted to mass possession is absent.

In reality, there are no guarantees in life; there are always uncertainties or risks involved in any action. If this is not recognized, then the individual enters a purely conceptual masque, where, instead of allowing life to live, everything is mentally ordered and rationalized. This involves one in the illusion that one is actually protected through the identification with the immortality symbols of others and of society.

Fear of death, then, is associated with systemic threats and rewards which, in turn, involve one in the mood of survival. Survival, however, is merely the perspective within which anxiety and isolation are manifested. The resort to rigidity, alienation and identification with authority are all, ultimately, attempts to control death ineffectively. The result is simply the inability to participate--thus one can become sufficiently driven to find meaning in the forbidding and harsh realities of war and revolution. It would seem that one, in a certain sense, must "free" oneself before one can free others.

In a manner of speaking, contemporary social science itself arose as the shared symbols degraded, and therefore cannot intentionally provide the new symbols within which people may find meaning since it has involved itself in the repression of the Self and a denial of the unconscious.

To identify with the state (or authority) in either an approach or avoidance manner involves dependence and an inability to participate, for the state is an illusion which, when identified with, makes its disruption a fearful thought to consider. It was Jung who wrote:

> The increasing dependence on the State is anything but
> a healthy symptom; it means that the whole nation is in
> a fair way to becoming a herd of sheep, constantly
> replying on a shepherd to drive them into good pastures.
> The shepherd's staff soon becomes a rod of iron, and
> the shepherds turn into wolves.[33]

The positive aspect of transference is that, as a partial actualization of Self, all objects of consciousness contain the truth which can be found if one is sincere and disciplined in the search. It is in this sense, that one always brings into being the "reality" required for Self discovery, even though that may mean the eventual death of the object, and, of the subject. ". . . the highest summit of life," Jung reflects, "can be expressed through the symbolism of death . . . for any growing beyond oneself means death."[34] That is the symbolic sacrifice necessary to dissolve the tyranny of the unconscious and to understand the wisdom of Phobos.

100

Notes for Chapter V

[1]Jung, Civilization in Transition, p. 408.

[2]Neumann, The Origins and History of Consciousness, pp. 390-391.

[3]Rank, Beyond Psychology, p. 21.

[4]Robert D. Hess and Judith V. Torney, The Development of Political Attitudes in Children (Chicago: Aldine Publishing Co., 1967).

[5]Bell and Edwards, American Government: The Facts Reorganized, p. 12.

[6]Rank, Beyond Psychology, p. 23.

[7]Ibid., pp. 26-27.

[8]Ibid., p. 31. This same perspective is found in Berger and Luckmann, The Social Construction of Reality, pp. 104ff. Neither Rank nor Berger and Luckmann, however, go beyond the personalistic aspects of the unconscious.

[9]Rank, Beyond Psychology, p. 40. Goethe said of nature that "The one thing she seems to aim at is Individuality; yet she cares nothing for individuals."

[10]Rank, Beyond Psychology, p. 41.

[11]Carl Becker, Modern Democracy, p. 33. Becker analyzes the foundations of the ideology of liberal democracy and its eventual division into conservative and liberal elements and notes that political power remained in the hands of upper-class parties regardless of the transference of power. Becker comments that

> an exceptionally able group of intellectuals who rationalized the social situation by identifying the middle-class interests and virtues with the rights of all men [appeared in western Europe]. (p. 39)

> . . . the interests of the bourgeoisie, both in the political and economic realm, proved in the long run to be in sharp conflict with the interests of the masses. It was the interest of the bourgeoisie to deny to the masses the political privileges which they demanded for themselves; while the freedom of economic enterprise which enriched bourgeois employers turned out to be,

for the proletarian peasants and workers, no more than the old subjection under new forms. (p. 41)

[12]Rank, Beyond Psychology, p. 43.

[13]Ibid., pp. 52-53.

[14]Ibid., p. 55.

[15]Ibid., p. 55.

[16]Jung, Civilization in Transition, pp. 486-487.

[17]Ibid., p. 696.

[18]Lt. William L. Calley, Jr., "The Confessions of Lieutenant Calley," Esquire, November 1970.

[19]Jung, Two Essays on Analytical Psychology, p. 139.

[20]Ibid., pp. 149-150.

[21]Neumann, The Origins and History of Consciousness, pp. 421-435.

[22]Jung, Two Essays on Analytical Psychology, p. 153.

[23]Ibid., p. 155.

[24]Ibid., p. 157.

[25]C. J. Jung, The Psychology of the Transference, Bollingen Series XX, Collected Works, vol. 16 (Princeton: Princeton University Press, 1969), p. xii.

[26]See: Gardner, Grendel. The monster sees through this problem in the formulation of "Grendel's law." "There is no limit to desire for desire's needs" (p. 80).

[27]Bruno Bettelheim, "Individual and Mass Behavior in Extreme Situations," Journal of Abnormal Social Psychology, 38 (1943):417-452. Bettelheim writes:

> A prisoner (speaking of the victims of German concentration camps) had reached the final stage of adjustment to the camp situation when he had changed his personality so as to accept as his own the values of the Gestapo . . . old prisoners were sometimes instrumental in getting rid of the unfit, in this way making a feature of Gestapo ideology a feature of their own behavior. (pp. 447-449)

[28] Jung, Two Essays on Analytical Psychology, p. 164.

[29] Ibid., p. 169.

[30] Ibid., p. 171.

[31] Jung elaborates in The Undiscovered Self upon authentic religion and its relation to the emancipation of the individual from the mass and to the individuation process. Discussed above is what Jung called creeds--a mass phenomenon.

[32] Singer, Boundaries of the Soul, pp. 114-115.

[33] Jung, Civilization in Transition, p. 413.

[34] C. G. Jung, Symbols of Transformation, Bollingen Series XX, Collected Works, vol. 5 (Princeton: Princeton University Press, 1967), p. 432.

CHAPTER VI

REFLECTIONS ON PHOBOS AND POLITICS

O judges, be of good cheer about death, and know of a
certainty, that no evil can happen to a good man, either
in life or after death. He and his are not neglected by
the gods; nor has my own approaching end happened by
mere chance.[1]

—Socrates

The etiology, inasmuch as one may speak of sources at all, of the
phenomena which have been portrayed to this juncture is threefold,
consisting of the mother complex, the problem of persona, and the
separation of consciousness and the unconscious. This trinary summation
is highly interrelated as, no doubt, will appear obvious to the reader. The
mother complex confounds the ability to see meaningful interconnections.
On the other hand, the Mother archetype, is the feminine side of God.
This archetype is to be highly treasured since she nourishes our lives. But
with the mother complex there arises everything that is regressive and
cheap in a human being. The mother complex is rebellious, regressive,
and reactive—it is a refusal to participate and reinforces the fear of
death. The complex is the giving up of individual responsibility.
Psychologically, it is "pure poison" as opposed to the "pure gold" of the
Mother archetype.[2] This complex is paradoxical inasmuch as it sets up
the tension that is necessary to the type of mental activity which
underlies the development of western science and technology. At the
same time, the great misfortune of the mother complex is that it carries
inflation with it as well. Ego-inflation is the arrogance of one's life; it
is knowing it all. It is very common for people to take something
beautiful which comes from the soul and feed the fires of hubris with it
when under the influence of the mother complex. The mother complex
can also carry ego-deflation with it which involves despair, depression,
crisis, and the questioning of the courage to live. In our time, many
philosophies and religions have been put forth with the promise of
overcoming such miseries and egotism. Some of these may, at first,
awaken the Mother archetype, but if the mother complex has not been
resolved, then it will eat up the sublime and turn it into hubris in a
regressive attempt to regain the Garden of Eden rather than moving
toward the authentic goal of life, that of Self-realization.

The problem of persona is the second characteristic of Phobos. The
concept of personhood is the prevalent vision of human beings in the
western world. Man is no longer considered to be a fragment of God, but
rather is individually responsible as a person, an independent agent, in his
relations with the world. The persona is maskedness so that relations

based in the notion of person, of self, of personality, are themselves masked. The identification with persona carries with it isolation, a lack of joy, and alienation. The persona problem is a detriment to interior life. It is stillborn of death. Since the singular focus on persona invites enantiodromia, the other side of personhood is tragedy. Both the mother complex and the problem of persona are associated with the separation of consciousness and the unconscious. The difficulty which comes from this separation has been elaborated upon considerably throughout this essay.

The social scientist, if he is to understand the life he studies, must resolve these three problems within himself: the mother complex; the problem of persona; and, the chasm between consciousness and the unconscious which arose with the intense rational differentiation of consciousness. Failure to pursue resolution turns science into a catamite for the unconscious. Self-knowledge, as opposed to knowledge of the ego-personality, should, in any case, be of primary importance to anyone who seeks to study or change other human beings or the world.

The view of Jung bears considerable significance for the under-standing of politics. Politics arises whenever disputes to authority occur. That is, we have politics when we have disputes concerning the nature of reality. Ontology is the foundation of politics. Authority sustains the prevalent vision of the nature of political reality. This is clearly a hermeneutical theme—all experience, political, social, and psychological is interpretation relative to an ontology. Power is the capacity to implement a particular construction of reality. This leads to the need to study the unconscious level of politics, for power is not merely armies, police, weapons, and money. Power has an unconscious dimension as well. Governments, in fact, rule most effectively at the unconscious level. This is where Jung is very helpful to the study of politics. In our time the great need is to study subliminal politics and such study must go hand in hand with Self-exploration.

Bureaucratization is symptomatic of the assimilation of the uncon-scious to the conscious rational mind. Socially speaking, we live in an organizational age which can provide no basis for community. Psycho-logically, people have developed a bureaucracy of mind—it is the same type of compartmentalization that can be seen in any government or large corporation. People tend to make bureaucratic ideology an aspect of their own psychology since they spend much of their time in institutional environments. Thus it becomes critical to see through ideology in all spheres of life, including the ideology which would characterize a politics of knowledge in the academic world. The methodological assumptions of a rationalistic social science must be thoroughly examined, particularly the notion of human nature and the notion that there are discoverable laws which regulate political and social events. For inherent in this latter conception is the idea that these laws should not be disturbed and that human beings ought to come into uniformity with them. This perspective, which excludes the unconscious, provides no place, in actuality, for the understanding of social and political phenomena. It eliminates the exercise of political philosophy and political art—it destroys the aesthetic dimension. In effect, the uncritical adoption of positivist and rational methodologies has subjected the social sciences to the forces of the unconscious. Thus it is that psychology has become an unconscious pursuit of personal integration, sociology of social integration or community, and political science of political community. Since the social sciences have not been self-examining, they remain impotent in their pursuits because they were born out of the disintegration of the archetypal canon; they arose from the dissolution of community and they represent that fact. In their rational and specialized quest, the social sciences often merely contribute to the bureaucratization of the individual mind.

The structure for integration is to be found within each individual, yet positive attitudes toward reflection, Self-knowledge, philosophy, and art which might illumine the search for community and integration are not particularly valued. In political terms, "society" now exerts control upon freedom, having replaced monarchy. And, it should be remembered that "society" includes not only governments, but also large-scale corporate enterprises. Much of what is to be considered political has already passed into the "private" arena, contributing further to the process of rendering politics unconscious and diffuse.

The Prospects for Change

At the same time the forces of rational control have grown, so have nonrational forces which have been manifested in the development of religious movements. The renewed interest in religion contains the possibility for both negative and positive change. Certainly the religion symbol represents the wholeness of the psyche as well as the brotherhood of man. Religion could awaken a consciousness of the common origin. Insofar as religion could sustain a concentration upon high goals, including: non-materialistic aims; freedom from selfish and ulterior considerations; compassion; and, the pursuit of justice; then positive integrative processes may be aroused within individuals which would be capable of dissolving and dispersing divisiveness. Notwithstanding, there is a great danger in the growth of religious forces for they may, if Jung's terms may be borrowed, be more apt to become creeds than religions as the mother complex devours them. There is evidence to support this negative assessment. The current Christian awakening, for instance, seems to be very closely aligned with materialistic considerations and ego-inflation. Christians have called for vastly increased arms spending in order to kill their brothers and sisters, have declared that God is a capitalist, and that economic salvation and spiritual salvation go hand in hand. Much of this religious fervor entails reactionary politics, visionary politics, patriotism, a regression to "old-time values," and a linking of religion with economics. Nelson Bunker Hunt, while attending a "Christian investment seminar," was reported to have said: "The most important thing to have is a spiritual environment in this country that will mean we can keep the money we can make."[3] Apparently God has a plan for making money. This point of view would not seem likely to encourage Self-knowledge or the withdrawal of divisive projections which might provide for a more peaceful political order domestically or internationally. Truly, such attitudes merely ensure, inasmuch as they are believed, that the times, particularly if they are characterized by political, social, and economic upheavals, will have an intense impact upon the unconscious. In this case, the need for a "leader" to "save" "the people" will emerge, and political authority and society will simply be based upon degraded religious symbols. This would be a time of inferior men. Some have, of course, judged them to be already in power.

If there is to be any change, that change must first occur within the individual. The individual must choose to pursue Self-realization since only in this manner may the individual maintain a steadfast attitude toward the pull of the collective archetypes of the herd. A healthy skepticism toward both political and religious ideology is a prerequisite. Substantive change cannot occur through the implementation of propaganda, indoctrination, advertising, socialization, religious injunctions, or economic and social engineering no matter in whose name such mass appeals are announced. The individual must consciously engage in the search for personal integration—it cannot be put upon the individual from the outside. The nation is a mirror of the psychology of those individuals who comprise it and only authentic changes within the individual can produce changes in it.

Politics in our time is a politics of fear—it is a fear derived from an ignorance of the unconscious and the primordial instincts of human beings as herd animals. Whether or not these instincts can be balanced or positively directed depends upon each individual. Socrates could serve as the symbol for us—the image of a man who, in his pursuit of truth, was liberated from the fear of death and who did not confuse Self-knowledge with knowledge of the ego-personality as is the wont of most human beings. One would hope that times are auspicious enough to allow us to understand, as did Socrates, that we know enough to know that we know nothing, and, yet, to marvel in that.

We all arise from the common sea which remains a profound mystery. Without this background, however, we could not so much as carry on a conversation. This must be recognized. The denial of the background upon which we individually dance, unearths the furies of the unconscious which, in their possessiveness, impell us to violently throw ourselves against the wall of unconsciousness over and over in terror and anger, bloodying and maiming ourselves and others in the frenzy. It is not the shadow man, but rather the heroic Socrates who nourishes us so that each one may have the courage to face death and live.

Notes for Chapter VI

[1]The Dialogues of Plato, translated by Benjamin Jowett (Chicago: Encyclopaedia Britannica, 1952), p. 211.

[2]I wish to note my indebtedness to Robert Johnson, a Jungian analyst, for his comments on this topic during the Conference on Western Psychotherapy and Eastern Religion sponsored by The Blaisdell Institute for the Advanced Study of World Cultures and Religions in June 1981, at Claremont, California. See also: Robert A. Johnson, He: Understanding Masculine Psychology (New York: Harper & Row, 1974); and Robert A. Johnson, She: Understanding Feminine Psychology (New York: Harper & Row, 1977).

[3]Russell Chandler, "God as Capitalist: Seminar Promotes Religion and Riches," Los Angeles Times, 1 June 1981, Pt. I, p. 3.